CAMPAIGN ORGANIZATION

Campaign Organization

Xandra Kayden

D. C. HEATH AND COMPANY
Lexington, Massachusetts   Toronto

To my mother

Preface

Studying campaign organizations is not unlike studying other kinds of organizations, and much of what can be said about campaigns can be said about any organized activity. Campaigns have certain special features owing to their temporary nature and to the heightened intensity of their activities. Their rewards are both tangible and important. But all organizations are political in the sense that they involve conflict among members, as individuals seek to derive benefits from the group or seek particular objectives for the group. The politicking that goes on in campaign organizations is no greater than that which might be found in other organizations, and may in fact be less because the outcomes of elections affect the real distribution of goods and services in society. Those who participate may defer the realization of their preferences until the election is won.

It may be that we pay little attention to the internal politics of campaigns because we are so concerned about their outcomes. Without for a moment suggesting that the substance of politics is unimportant, it does seem to me that more attention to the process is in order, particularly as we address issues of campaign reform.

The following pages describe campaigns as organizations: their membership, their efforts to ensure their maintenance, and their attempts to influence the electorate. The book also includes an analysis of the media, particularly the media's organizational nature, with an eye toward understanding the constraints under which members of different organizations operate and the ways in which those constraints affect their perceptions and actions. Much of what a campaign organization does to elect its candidate becomes obscured by the interpretations of others — notably the media. And much of what a campaign does to attract attention to itself goes unnoticed because the electorate is bored, is looking elsewhere, or is content to make a choice along party lines after all.

The three campaigns that form the basis of this book were each studied for a period of two weeks during the 1974 campaign season, from mid-September to November. They were selected to be as different from each other as possible in order to learn what was similar about them. The differences were external, relating to the status of the political parties, the offices sought, the length of each candidate's service in office, and peculiarities of political culture due to geographic and historic differences.

There were two Republican gubernatorial campaigns: the effort to re-elect Governor Francis W. Sargent in Massachusetts; and the campaign of Lamar Alexander in Tennessee, a state where the governor cannot succeed himself. In Massachusetts, the Republicans were in the minority and likely to remain so. In Tennessee, the Republicans were in the ascendancy, having captured all of the statewide offices in the last ten years and a majority of the congressional delegation as well. The Indiana race was the re-election campaign of United States Senator Birch Bayh, a Democrat from a state known for the strength of both parties.

Although I spent much of my time interviewing members of the campaign staffs and asking them similar questions about their backgrounds and their roles in the campaigns, much of what I learned came from spending time with the organizations and watching the interaction that goes on on a daily basis. It took a week for me to get to know all the people in a campaign and for them to begin to feel comfortable having me around. By the beginning of the second week, I was becoming part of the organization to the extent that I had a sense of what was happening and would be included in most organizational debates. The intensities of campaigns are such that had I stayed much beyond the second week, I would have become involved in the struggles going on within the organization. It was just as well I had to move on to another campaign, though I returned to each a few days before the election.

The methodology used in this study is suited to the complexities and nuances of small-group behavior. Becoming part of the group enabled me to learn what concerned those I studied, not what I thought ought to concern them. And moving from group to group enabled me to see patterns I might otherwise have ascribed to the idiosyncrasies of one individual or one·organization. Proof, in this approach, does not rest in numbers, but in common sense and in the belief that another observer studying the same subject would draw similar conclusions. Ultimately, of course, it rests in the credibility of the researcher.

Many things have been said about the 1974 election and its significance for parties and voters alike, most of which have to do with reaction to scandal in the White House and the state of the economy. However, the issues discussed in these particular campaigns were not the issues to which the national media paid attention. Some issues were of state interest, such as taxes and prison reform. Some related to more general problems, such as abortion and gun control. As far as an observer could tell, however, these campaigns could have taken place in 1970 and probably in 1980.

As writing projects go, this was a very happy experience, made so by the interest and support of a number of people. James Q. Wilson was an ideal advisor and teacher throughout my career at Harvard. I cannot imagine a more perfectly suited match of interests and approach. The project was made possible by the strong support of Robert Goldmann and William Grinker of the Ford Foundation. Their interest and advice, particularly Mr. Goldmann's, who became the project officer for the foundation, was important to me throughout. Jonathan Moore, an old friend and director of the Institute of Politics of the John F. Kennedy School of Government at Harvard, made it possible for me to complete the work in the warm environment of the Institute. I am indebted to him and the Institute's staff. In addition, I greatly appreciate the interest of Professors Richard E. Neustadt, William Schneider, and Abraham Zaleznik, and that of Stephen Hess and Milton Gwirtzman, experienced political writers. I would also like to thank Suzanne Hilton of the Institute, who administered the grant, and Marcessia Gelowtski, who typed the manuscript.

Needless to say, a study of campaign organizations would not have been possible without the interest and cooperation of those studied. People to whom I feel a particular debt are Gary Sisco, Tom Beasley, Fairia Davidson, and Marc Levene in Tennessee; Jason Berman, David Bochnowski, P. A. Mack, Susan Williams, and Allen Dale in Indiana; and Steve Crosby, Al Kramer, Judy Meredith, and Tom Reardon in Massachusetts. Jack Flannery, Chief Secretary to Governor Sargent, was helpful throughout the project. And there are, of course, the candidates, who showed patience and forbearance: Lamar Alexander, Francis W. Sargent, and Birch Bayh, who noted that he was pleased to have me along to observe, even though he was not quite sure what it was I was observing.

Since I did not embark upon this study with many preconceptions, it would only be fair to say that what I learned, I learned because almost everyone I met was willing to let me see things happen without knowing how they would turn out, or without knowing what I would choose to report upon. Given the nature of politics, that requires trust and confidence in themselves as well as me, for which I am very thankful indeed.

X.K.

Cambridge, Massachusetts

Contents

Chapter 1

Introduction

A campaign may make the difference between winning and losing an election, but very few people outside politics know what a campaign organization does. This book is an analytic description of campaign organizations and of the impact of the environment of those organizations on the people who participate in them.

The significance of questions about campaigns is obvious: democratic societies are premised on free elections. By "free," I mean an open process that enables voters to make informed choices among candidates for office. There are those who argue that this competition for leadership is *the* distinctive feature of a democracy.[1] If there is something inherent in campaigns that obscures openness, we ought to know about it. If there is something inherent in campaigns that makes certain

---

[1] E.g., Joseph Schumpeter, *Capitalism, Socialism and Democracy* (New York: Harper & Brothers, 1942), and Robert Dahl, *Preface to Democratic Theory* (Chicago: University of Chicago Press, 1956).

kinds of behavior inevitable, we ought to be aware of it so that we can construct our laws and regulations in ways that will achieve the ends we seek. And of course, if there is something in campaigns that affects what voters perceive about a candidate, we ought to seek an understanding of it so that we can better educate ourselves, thereby assuring a freer, more open electoral process.

Politics is a complex and fascinating process. This book is about process more than substance. I am concerned here more with how people made decisions than with what decisions were made. The book is about people: what people choose to participate in campaigns; what kinds of beliefs they bring with them; what kinds of expectations they hold for themselves as a result of their participation. It is about the environment to which these people come and how that environment affects, or fails to affect, those perceptions and expectations. Somebody in one of the campaigns studied said, "When you work sixteen hours a day, seven days a week, something happens." This book is about what happens.

Before taking a closer look at the campaigns studied, there are some generalizations to be made about them, particularly about those topics that appear to be given short shrift in the book: the candidate and the election.

The Nature of Campaigns

Politics is a fairly traditional activity in America. One reason, perhaps the most important reason, is the complexity and uncertainty of the political environment. If something worked in the past, we expect it will probably work in the future; because of the uncertainty, however, we can never really be sure just what it was that did work in the past. Did Senator Jones win re-election because of his voting record, or because of his media campaign? Tradition tends to include everything that was ever done (or at least remembered). It is almost synonymous with superstition. If the candidate made an appearance at a pancake breakfast during his last campaign, he certainly will not miss it this time. Another reason for the importance of tradition is the belief, held strongly by political actors, that they should represent the dominant — the traditional — attitudes and mores of the society. Tradition is valued for its own sake.

While politics tends toward the traditional, there are urgent pressures to encompass newer worlds: new issues, new constituencies, sometimes even new ways of doing things. There can be conflict between the old and the new, as well as other kinds of conflicts. There are always questions as to the proper distribution of goods and services in an election, and campaign organizations address such questions in a way that will enable the candidate to put together the largest possible coalition of supporters.

Issues and issue-constituencies are the objects for which campaigns bid. The trick is to put together the right collection of issues so that one constituency is not alienated by another constituency. American politics is not particularly ideological, but there are sets of issues that fall into general categories of liberalism and conservatism, and even though the issues may not logically follow one another in a conservative or liberal progression, few campaigns will try to mix them. Conflicts exist particularly when new issues and groups seek recognition and priority over older, more established issues and groups.

It is the strength, perhaps the genius, of political campaigns that they are able to meet many of the conflicting demands set upon them. They are temporary, complex organizations that have one object: getting the candidate elected. There is no second place. The closer the election gets, the more flexible the organization becomes in seeking compromise and blending the new and the old.

The Campaign and the Candidate

The candidate, the raison d'être for a campaign organization, is not really a member of the organization as such. He or she may play a large role in the selection of the campaign staff and be the final arbiter in struggles among the staff, but a candidate is not so much a member as an object of the organization. This is particularly true because the candidate is usually out on the road and not part of the day-to-day or minute-by-minute crises. It is also true that there is a decided tendency to depersonalize the commitment made by individuals to the candidate as an individual.

We are very uneasy in America about committing ourselves to another person. There are, in fact, few fields where such a commitment is made publicly and strongly. Politics is one, the entertainment field another. In campaigns, a depersonalization takes place and staff members will speak of "the Candidate," "the Boss," "the Senator," "the Governor," and so on. They will come to think of their candidate as a body that gets moved around from place to place and says the lines he or she is told to say. If a line is missed or an impromptu one inserted, it increases the sense of frustration felt by some in the organization.

In the campaigns studied here where the candidate was an incumbent, there was a stronger sense of him as an individual and undoubtedly a stronger relationship between the candidate and his staff members. In the organizations created new for the campaign, however, the candidate was often an image to most of the staff, an image who was usually idealized and occasionally decried. A secretary in Tennessee who tended toward extremes spoke of Lamar Alexander as "a breath of fresh air. When he comes into the office I feel as if ten tons had been lifted off my shoulders." The farther away staff members were from the top of the organization, the more idealized the candidate became, and perhaps the less valued the staff became. One volunteer in the Bayh organization accused his regular Senate staff: "Birch Bayh is a great senator with a mediocre staff. There's no sense of commitment to Bayh. It's almost as if they really don't believe in him and aren't committed. Almost an 'oh well, we're going to do this' attitude." To the Bayh staff, however, charismatic appeal and idealization of the candidate were inappropriate.

Staff attitudes toward the candidate reflect, at least in part, the candidate's attitude toward the staff. Birch Bayh tried to avoid the special treatment that charisma engenders. Francis Sargent, who liked the special treatment accorded a governor, surrounded himself with people who would disagree with each other, but who did so with humor and irreverence for the circumstances. They created a special environment around the governor.

Candor and irreverence are qualities the candidates spoke of when they talked about what they looked for in a staff. All three said they wanted honesty in a staff member: the ability to differentiate reality from gossip and to speak up about it. Uncertainty is a fact of life in politics. Those who make the most noise can, and often do, represent a very small interest group. Politicians tend to preserve their options and do not often take positions early in a discussion. Information about which side someone will be on, or how many will be on a side, can be valuable. The ability to discern the truth, to understand the nuances of political jargon, appears to be among the most important attributes a staff member has to recommend himself or herself to a candidate.

Another important quality is loyalty, perhaps a peculiar political kind of loyalty that can almost be measured in favors given and received. It was the first quality mentioned by Bayh, and it is not therefore surprising that almost all of his staff began working for him when they were interns in college and never left his office. Most of those who left did so because they left Washington.

Why People Work in Campaigns

Politics is a peculiarly demanding area of human activity. It draws people to it for a variety of reasons, and it is important to understand those reasons because of the significance of the activity. Although we have a strong antipolitical tradition in this country, not only are people drawn to the political arena, they fight to get in and to keep others out. There is a certain mystery to the exercise of power and there is no field of endeavor in which power is used so nakedly.[2] Over and over again people spoke of being consumed by the campaigns in which they worked. Part of the reason was easy to discern: the complete dedication of time and energy they made to the organization, a dedication that required cutting away of other ties. But part of the reason was the excitement political activity generates in

---

[2]Harold Lasswell, *Power and Personality* (New York: Viking, 1962), and *Power and Society* (New Haven: Yale University Press, 1950).

those who participate in it, an excitement due to the expectation of holding power.

Power is an important reward; another is the sense of belonging. A campaign is, after all, a battle waged with clearly marked sides and a definite winner. It is more or less cilvilized warfare, and it is emotionally rewarding. It is not so much the battle that is the source of the reward, I think, as it is the sense of being part of a team. This group focus may be particularly common among the new generation of political actors who grew up during the great societal movements and had strong feelings about group solidarity (described in Chapter Three). Alliances among individuals occur frequently within campaigns — not necessarily to the good of the organization — but the tendency for two people to form an alliance is only one manifestation of a larger need to be part of something.

Political campaigns can fulfill what might be called a symbolic need to belong to the society, to be part of things. A campaign is symbolic in the sense that it is what people expect elections to be about: one team against another. For those whose relationship to the campaign is only peripheral, and whose expectations are not altered because they are only peripheral, the campaign is a team effort against another team. Those who are full-time members of the organizations still carry with them that sense of belonging, but the focus of opposition shifts from the candidate of the other party to people within their own campaign organization. Alliances are formed against others in the organization. Sometimes the alliances are formed along task lines, sometimes they transcend tasks, often they form along lines of physical proximity: those who work in the same room are suspicious of those who work in another room or another side of the building.

Aside from the attractions of power and belonging, many participate in campaigns because participation enables people to perform their duty as citizens. For some that service need be no more than volunteering once or twice in a campaign; for others, it means taking a year or two out of one's life and devoting it to public service. Though most of us derive a sense of civic satisfaction from voting, some feel a greater need to participate in public life.[3]

Power and the sense of belonging are rewards that come only after one has become part of the political world. I suspect there is a deep psychological basis for this sense of public-mindedness. Those who have it would seem to have wide horizons and see a relationship between themselves as individuals and public events. All societies are dependent upon this sense of responsibility or civic-mindedness; none more than democracies. Yet there are personal costs to participation in political life. Private relationships probably suffer the most, along with the time for leisure activities and reflection. Public sacrifice may also include the sacrifice of honor, sometimes justified, sometimes not.

The following pages do not dwell heavily on the psychological motivation of political actors, although there are some obvious conclusions that can be drawn about where they are in the life cycle and the consequences of that in the roles they perform in campaigns. Those at the beginning and end of the life cycle have more time, and perhaps more need, to participate in something as dynamic as a political campaign. Those in the prime of life may have more of an expectation of reward, partly because their sacrifice may be greater in relation to their daily life, and partly because they came of age politically at a time when reward was to be expected.

Campaign Styles

Differences could be discerned among the three campaigns in this study, but they did not turn out to be based on party, ideology, office sought, or incumbency. Although candidates are generally peripheral to the campaign organization, it was possible here to categorize the campaigns by the degree to which the organization was responsive to the candidate: Organizations whose members reflected the personal style of the

---

[3]Sidney Verba and Norman H. Nie, *Participation in American Political Democracy and Social Equality* (New York: Harper and Row, 1972), 85.

candidate more than they did the tasks of the organization or the character of the party or state can be called *personalized* campaigns; organizations whose members reflected the tasks they performed more than the style of the candidate and maintained some distance between themselves and their roles in the organization can be called *professionalized* campaigns.

The Personalized Campaign

The campaign of Lamar Alexander in Tennessee was representative of the personalized campaign. The professional staff was carefully selected by the candidate from people of relatively similar background, education, and political experience. Both the candidate and the campaign consultant spoke of the staff as a group of young people who had the ability to learn how to campaign from the candidate (who had been a campaign manager himself) and who would accept the candidate's ideas. As one observer noted of the staff, "They knew enough about politics to know the people and the situations, but they don't operate from a sense of their own power or constituency. Without a proven area of campaign competence, they don't feel they are indispensable and are therefore more malleable and amenable to the candidate's direction and the forming of a cohesive organization."

Both Republican campaign organizations appeared relatively homogeneous compared to the Democratic organization of Birch Bayh. Alexander's was even more homogeneous than Sargent's, possibly because of the greater diversity in the Massachusetts electorate. In any case, the Alexander staff was, on the average, in their middle twenties, had attended the state university, had worked in marginal capacities in other campaigns, and had a low-keyed personal style that was very much akin to the candidate's. Many of them felt a sense of civic duty or idealism as a basis for their participation in politics, but more were aware that they could afford to take the time for participation at this point in their lives — a point before they had to "get serious" about a career.

The strength of the personalized campaign is its homogeneity. Communication is perhaps the one consistently difficult problem for any organization to solve. A complex temporary organization such as a political campaign has that problem in extreme form. The homogeneity of a personalized campaign eases communication problems because, at the very least, most organization members have a common base of experience and a common language.

One weakness of a personalized campaign is the tendency of its members to be generalists and to expect to participate in all decision making. Knowing that those performing other tasks have no special qualifications for them, campaign members tended to interfere more with decisions in areas other than their own. In fact, if people knew decisions were going to be made, they wanted to be included in the process, slowing it considerably. Another weakness of a personalized campaign (perhaps, in certain circumstances, a strength) is the sharp distinction made between those who belong to the organization and those who do not. Outsiders stand out clearly. It may not be in the best interest of a political campaign to have such an obvious line between who is in and who is out.

The Professionalized Campaign

The Bayh campaign was representative of a professionalized campaign organization in its distribution of tasks, its use of new techniques (such as special programs for involving volunteers, and computer technology), and the sense of distance the staff members had from their roles within the organization and from the candidate. There was, of course, a clear personal commitment to Senator Bayh, such as is characteristic of political campaigns, but neither he nor his opponent was blown up to be a larger-than-life representative of good or evil. Loyalty to the candidate was expected and received, but it was that peculiar political loyalty that is the first tenet of a code of behavior characteristic of traditional politics in America.

Professionalism, in the classic sense of the term, can be applied to the Bayh campaign organization, except that there are several characteristics of its membership that do not fit into accepted definitions of the term.[4] Campaign members were

---

[4]Peter L. Blau and W. Richard Scott, *Formal Organizations* (San Francisco: Chandler, 1961), 60–74.

not specifically trained, able to produce credentials, or mobile. They were, in fact, surprisingly immobile in the sense that most members of the campaign staff had spent their entire professional lives working for Birch Bayh. They were professional in the sense of having a specialized task orientation (rather than the generalist orientation of the Alexander campaign) and in the distance they placed between themselves, the candidate, and the organization. They were also professional in their awareness of new techniques in the field and their willingness to experiment with them.

In contrast to the personalized campaign, the strength of the professionalized organization is its ability to allocate responsibilities according to tasks and allow decisions to be made by those in charge of them. Conflicts between tasks (some of which will be seen to be inherent in campaigning) were settled higher up in the organizational hierarchy, but they appeared to occur less frequently in Indiana than they did in Tennessee. The value of a focus on tasks in campaigns is that most tasks lend themselves to measures of one sort or another, and even though it is difficult — if not impossible — to relate those measures to the likelihood of success or failure at the polls, having them enables members of the organization to set goals for themselves and to lessen the uncertainty of the environment in which they live.

The difficulty of a professionalized campaign is that it adds to the communications problems because people working on one task will have very little knowledge of what others in the organization are doing. The danger of suboptimization is considerable in these circumstances.[5] As one member of the Indiana campaign noted, "The science of politics is to break down the tasks. The problem is that after they're broken down — how do you put them back for the whole task?" The problem of communication is compounded since people are

[5]Suboptimization occurs when people working at lower levels in an organization do not hold the same values as those at the top and, in the words of Hitch and McKean, "they attempt to find optimal (or near-optimal) solutions, but to subproblems rather than to the whole problem of the organization." Charles J. Hitch and Roland McKean, *The Economics of Defense in the Nuclear Age* (Cambridge: Harvard University Press, 1960), Chapter 12.

selected because of their ability to perform tasks, not their common background or their similarity to the candidate.

This stress upon a common language may seem excessive, but it should be borne in mind that campaigns are intense, fast-moving organizations with a limited time frame. As temporary organizations they do not have the luxury of learning by trial and error; perhaps they do not have the luxury of learning at all. People are hired to perform tasks and it is very hard to judge whether or not those tasks are being performed well. People are measured by the time they spend at headquarters, by the number of telephone calls they receive, or the amount of mail addressed to them, and so on — all measures that may relate to the structure in which they are operating, but not to the substance of their work.

The Massachusetts campaign of Francis Sargent combined characteristics of both the personalized and the professionalized campaigns, partly because it consisted of two organizations: the staff in the statehouse and the separate campaign organization. Because Sargent was the incumbent governor, the campaign was never entirely separate from the administration. Although Bayh was also an incumbent, for all practical purposes his activity in Indiana was related solely to the campaign, and the members of his Senate staff who served in the campaign were officially transferred to the campaign payroll and had little to do with their Washington tasks during the campaign period.

This characterization of campaigns according to their personalized or professionalized nature is helpful in understanding variations in style of decision making between campaigns, but it is not sufficient to explain campaigns. If there is any single rule that dominates political decision making it is this: *decisions are made by whoever happens to be in the room at the time.* And if one were to generalize about campaign conflicts, considerable weight must be given to the kinds of tasks campaigns perform: those that call for skill in handling people and those that call for careful methodical measures. The former require a high tolerance for ambiguity; the latter, an orientation toward efficiency. Campaigns work more smoothly if the right people are in the right tasks.

This study is about campaign organizations more than it is about campaigns. Winning or losing the election is after the fact. The members of all three campaigns believed they were going to win. One should never underestimate the ability of people to convince themselves of what they want to believe in any circumstance. Campaign members are particularly prone to wishful thinking because they exist in an extremely uncertain environment, because the members of the staff talk almost exclusively to their own supporters, and because they believe in miracles. Many of the factors that influence elections are well beyond the scope of the campaign (the state of the economy, attitudes about the administration in Washington, actions by the President during the course of the campaign, local events like the busing crisis in Boston, and so on). None of the organizations could or would have acted very differently had they known the outcome ahead of time, had their isolation from the rest of political life been any less profound. It is, therefore, only of marginal interest to note that Birch Bayh was the one candidate in the study to win his election.[6]

The rewards people find in political activity outweigh the costs, but they are harder to describe. The following chapters will explain the kinds of tensions that campaign organizations engender; they will dwell only casually on the kinds of joys participants derive. Campaigns are very compelling experiences, regardless of the outcome of the election. They are exciting because they are an important part of the political process and much of what they do is instantly reported in television and in the newspapers, adding to that sense of immediacy and significance.

---

[6]The election results were as follows:

Tennessee	Lamar Alexander	458,320 (44.1%)
	Ray Blanton	581,671 (55.9%)
Indiana	Birch Bayh	844,770 (51.6%)
	Richard Lugar	793,730 (48.4%)
Massachusetts	Francis Sargent	766,611 (44.1%)
	Michael Dukakis	970,582 (55.9%)

It is interesting to note that Alexander and Sargent, the two Republican candidates, polled the same percentage of the vote in their states.

Chapter 2

The Campaigns

Because there is such a thing as a season, and because politics is so bound by tradition, there is a typical rhythm to campaigns. There are many things to do and the sorting out of priorities occurs in September and early October. October is the busiest time, when commitments are either met or discarded, and as the election draws near the work load decreases in the central campaign headquarters and the anxiety increases. It makes a difference, therefore, when one looks at a campaign. Bearing that rhythm in mind, you could almost read the following organizational descriptions as the story of one campaign instead of three separate and entirely different races. Disputes in one organization may have resembled those that happened in another at the same time, but whether they did or not, each campaign at each period had some organizational crisis to solve. How each solved it explains much about these campaigns in particular and all campaigns in general.

Each of the campaign organizations was studied for a two-week period, beginning with Tennessee in the last half of September and ending with Massachusetts. The serious political "season" is generally considered to begin after Labor Day and build momentum until the election in early November. All three campaign organizations had been in existence many months before (Tennessee and Massachusetts both had primaries to win), but theoretically at least full-scale operations did not begin until September.

Tennessee

The Republican nominee in Tennessee was the surprise victor in an August primary. Lamar Alexander was a thirty-four-year-old attorney who had played a leading staff role in the election of other successful Republicans in the state. He was running against the Democratic nominee, Ray Blanton, a former congressman who had made one statewide race before when he ran for the Senate against Howard Baker in 1972. This was Alexander's first experience as a candidate, and he brought to it much of his understanding of campaign organizations and Tennessee politics. He chose his staff carefully, beginning eight months before the primary in January of 1974. The strong resemblance between himself and the staff was a mark of his care and, as it turns out, a mark of a personalized campaign organization.

Republican politics in Tennessee was only ten years old as a statewide phenomenon, though it had existed for generations in the mountainous eastern part of the state. By the time of the gubernatorial race, the Republicans had elected two United States senators (Howard Baker and Bill Brock), five out of eight congressmen, and, for the first time in almost fifty years, a governor. As in many southern states, the governor cannot succeed himself, and this election was thought by many to be a test of the strength of the statewide party and its ability to pass along the reins of power. Factionalism, which is common in southern Democratic politics — as in any party that has dominated a state for a long period of time — could affect as well the new-found strength of the Republicans. Tennessee was considered a bellwether of the changing political scene. For Tennessee Republicans, there was also a question of whether or not the party could buck the national trend back to a Democratic majority.

The objective of the campaign was to win the election of a relatively unknown young man and to avoid splitting the party. This was an obvious problem in the general election because there had been four candidates in the Republican primary, each with his own organization. The winner was inevitably left with the problem of putting all these politically active people back together. It was not unlike the problem of Humpty Dumpty, though the king's horsemen may have had the advantage in at least knowing which of the things lying around on the ground were part of the egg. The Alexander organization had trouble knowing who the participants were in the organizations of their opponents and whether or not those people should be brought into their own campaign. There were also ideological differences among the candidates in the primary; reaching out to the backers of the more conservative candidate was a problem. The campaign strategy was a "mix between a heavy organizational effort and a significant effort with the media."[1]

The media strategy was necessary because Alexander, although known inside the party, was not known to the voters. Because of the geographic peculiarities of Tennessee (a short, wide strip of land with three distinct sections), there were five major media markets: Tri-Cities, Knoxville, Nashville, Chattanooga, and Memphis. The candidate was scheduled to fly into each of these areas with increasing frequency as the campaign wore on. Alexander also met with newspaper people across the state: the local weeklies had played a major role in the primary victory when their endorsements helped the electorate choose among a crowded candidate field. Of the three campaigns studied, the Tennessee race placed least emphasis on television and most on newspapers, partly because of the success in gaining newspaper endorsements in the primary, and perhaps because Alexander and his press secretary had both been newspaper reporters and had a better feel for that kind of medium.

---

[1] Interview with Hal Carter, Tennessee campaign chairman, September 23, 1974.

Campaign strategy was also responsive to the political differences in the state, which parallel the geography. The east is clearly Republican and has been since the Civil War. In order to carry the state, Alexander would need a heavy turnout in this mountainous country. It was also the base of the primary's more conservative candidate, and much of the traditional leadership in the party had been with the opposition and needed to be brought back to the fold for the general election. The middle part of the state is probably the most solidly Democratic section, and here the campaign sought to establish a highly visible field organization that would, as one participant put it, "drive Ray Blanton out of his skull." The western part of Tennessee is dominated politically by Memphis; the Republican strategy was to wean away as much of the black vote as it could garner without at the same time alienating the traditional white racist vote in the area. As one staff member put it, it was a question of whether they "weren't going to swap the devil for his grandmother."

This, then, was the political environment in which the campaign for governor was set. Factionalism was a serious problem, but one that was at least anticipated; those who coordinated the field organization for the campaign were clearly chosen for that task and were, as a group, older and more representative of the diversity within the party than the rest of the staff. The anonymity of the candidate was compounded by geography and by the historic political divisions, which left no city (or its media market) dominant, thus requiring constant travel to maintain visibility.

During the period of the study (the last two weeks of September), there were two major organizational issues or problems: First, there was the decision-making process in the organization, particularly when it came to setting the schedule; and second, the handling of problems in the field when one group of volunteers would oppose other groups of volunteers, usually along the lines of who had been with which candidate in the primary. The scheduling problem was compounded by the campaign strategy, which was, at the time, to have Alexander appear on the same platform with his opponent. It was not a direct challenge for debate that Alexander was seeking because, as one aide noted, a direct challenge could lead to a direct answer: no. This "debate-chase strategy" was successful in drawing media attention to Alexander's willingness to debate his opponent, or at least appear on the same platform so people could ask questions of them both, and it was particularly successful in showing Blanton canceling appearances in order to avoid such a meeting. By the end of the study the two candidates did appear on the same platform and Alexander did extend a formal challenge to debate. Blanton refused, citing Alexander's unwillingness to talk about the issues. This was followed by a press conference in which Alexander listed ten issues on which they disagreed and could debate, but the campaign moved in other directions, and the staff began to have second thoughts about the costs to their organization of such a strategy.

A major problem had been keeping the candidate's schedule flexible enough to enable him to make last-minute appearances where Blanton was scheduled to speak, which prevented the organization from making commitments to its own supporters for the candidate's time. Because decisions were slow in coming, more and more people within the organization were involved in them, and midway through the study there were serious challenges to the process by competing task groups (the field organization, the finance and press departments).

Another problem with the debate-chase strategy was that members of the Alexander organization became absorbed in the doings of their opponent and several began to feel they were losing their own momentum. This may have been compounded by the physical setting: the Alexander campaign headquarters was situated on a highway outside of Nashville next door to the Blanton headquarters. Every time anyone went in or out of either headquarters, people would notice the cars parked in front of the opponent's building, wondering who was inside and why. Whatever the cause of the focus on Blanton, it appeared to be draining much of the staff energy in the last half of September. When they recognized what was happening, several members of the staff felt it was time to turn over a new leaf in the campaign and focus on the strength of their own candidate rather than the weakness of his opponent.

The emotional involvement in the race by the campaign staff may also have been due to the personalities of both candidates and to the nature of the group. According to Alexander, he had sought to surround himself with people who were capable, who had worked for the Republican party (though there were exceptions), who would accept his ideas, and who could learn. He wanted people who "had the capability of recognizing problems and handling diverse problems under pressure, and who had the ability to tell the truth."[2]

The campaign organization that resulted was "unique," in the eyes of the professional campaign consultant, because it was young and therefore better able to handle the new political technology than old-timers have been (although as it turned out the age of these campaign members corresponded to their counterparts in Indiana and Massachusetts), and it was a reflection of Alexander's ideas.[3] With few exceptions, no one in the organization had previously held positions of responsibility in campaigns. The candidate felt they would learn in the primary and be able to function on their own in the general election (a questionable assumption because the primary race was different from the general election, with only two candidates). It was also suggested by some that by taking on new people, the candidate would be creating his own organization — people loyal to him instead of to party factions.

A consequence of this new experience with responsibility was that the staff did not appear especially power-oriented. One theme of the study (to be developed in a later chapter) is that those closest to the core of an organization are the least likely to express a power concern, whereas the farther away from that core people are, the more likely they are to have an exaggerated sense of the rules of the game in politics and the exercise of power. It could also be that, because the Republican party was so young in Tennessee, those at the campaign level were still imbued with the sense of idealism that comes

---

[2]Interview with Lamar Alexander, September 30, 1974.

[3]Interview with Clifford White, Tennessee campaign consultant, September 23, 1974.

from the founding of an organization and were not yet accustomed to the expectation of spoils that comes from winning office. Still another possible explanation — one that holds true for this entire generation of political actors — is that those who are participating in politics today have a strong sense of personal efficacy and do not feel so great a need to use their participation as a tool to further their careers. They believe they will be successful in or out of politics, and that, although it might be nice to work for the governor, the opportunity would exist for them whether or not they participated in the campaign.

The careful selection of the professional staff and the strong resemblance between the candidate and that staff did not reach down to the clerical support level of the campaign organization, and there were some interesting consequences of the differences between these two groups of people. All three campaign organizations had serious conflicts between the professional and the clerical staffs, but perhaps they were particularly obvious in Tennessee because of the greater homogeneity at the top, including the greater likelihood of men being in professional roles and women in support roles.

Most of the professional staff were in their middle twenties, single, and graduates of the University of Tennessee. The campaign expanded after the primary to include people who were slightly older and married, and who had worked for the losing candidates. Several of those who came late to the organization spoke of the need they felt not to interfere with the dominant style and decision-making process, which forced decisions upward in the organization to be made by the campaign manager or the candidate himself. The process worked because it was not put under too much stress by campaign members; people accepted the decisions that came down, or at least most of them did. The newcomers to the organization made conscious decisions not to upset that balance.

During the study a problem was created when a party county chairperson in the field appointed a three-person committee to head the campaign for the general election. The problem was not so much who was on the committee but that the county chairperson made the appointments without consulting anyone — notably omitting the man who had led the candidate's campaign in the primary. Alexander's early supporter had been promised by a member of the field organization that he would not be forgotten in the general election. When the announcement of the committee was made public, the early supporters objected, and the county chairperson said he would resign unless he were backed up by the campaign. The issue was complicated by the friendship between the county chairperson and the finance chairperson in the area. If the former resigned, how many people would follow him, and would the campaign also lose its county finance chairperson?

The field organization staff (two of whom were being played off against each other, because the county chairperson was citing one and the early supporters were citing another) went to the campaign manager with the problem. He, in turn, went to the head of the finance department, whose response was initially that he wanted to be kept out of political disputes and secondly that the local finance chairperson "will not want to sit it out." The campaign manager reminded the head of the finance department that he had earlier complained of not being kept well enough informed on political matters, and asked him to call the local finance person because "it would make him feel better to be consulted about it before anything happens." The campaign manager waited most of the day for the head of the finance department to make the telephone call, and when that failed, he met with the field organization people and decided to let the county chairperson resign, saying finally, "There aren't enough of our supporters in that county to worry about this."

The campaign manager's handling of the issue was to raise it with the staff people involved and let them mull it over for awhile before deciding to let things take their own course. Although he ultimately supported the field staff's view that the county chairperson should be let go, he seemed unaware of how seriously the field staff people took this challenge to their professional reputations. One of the field people noted, "If the campaign manager had gone the other way, he would have had a fight on his hands. My personal integrity was involved because I had gone down to the county and organized in the primary and told people I got they would stick through the general election. It's a matter of principle, and you don't forsake principles for politics. It's like the expression 'his word is his bond.' I guard my integrity with my life."

The issue did not end there, however, because a few days later the local finance chairperson met with the head of the finance department and argued against the early supporters of the candidate in the primary. The head of the finance department came to the field staff people the next day complaining that "all the better people moved out." They talked for awhile about how they could tell who the "better people" really were, and the head of the field staff closed the discussion saying, "We can't drop people, and we're past the point of crying about it. We're past the point of worrying about 2200 votes."

In terms of the campaign organization, the issue never really was resolved; things just moved on. The members of the field staff would talk about it from time to time, and doubtless it was a topic of conversation in the county, but the question of integrity and support, which was very much an issue for the field people, was never raised with either the campaign manager or the head of the finance department. According to the campaign manager, even if he had been aware of the personal way in which his staff was responding to the threat to its integrity, there was a limit to how responsive he could be. It was his decision, and he had to get the job done as well as possible for the candidate.

Indiana

"If you like politics, you'll love Indiana." Unlike almost every other state in the Union, Indiana has a strong two-party system that is heavily financed by legal kickbacks from all political appointees.[4] As long as there is an equitable distribution of offices, there will be an equitable distribution of organizational strength between the parties. The race for the United States Senate between Birch Bayh (incumbent Democrat) and Richard

---

[4] Recent federal law prohibits Indiana from continuing its kickback system.

Lugar (Republican mayor of Indianapolis) was thought from the beginning to be a close conflict between two good candidates, each of whom had national aspirations weighing on the outcome.

One of the reasons for equality between the parties is the demographic makeup of the state. Southern Indiana is rural, conservative, and largely Republican. The Ku Klux Klan, it will be remembered, was strong in Indiana. The northern section of the state, part of which borders Chicago, is urban and heavily industrialized, with large black and ethnic populations. Unions play an important role in Democratic politics within the state, particularly the United Auto Workers, which includes in its bylaws a rule that all officers must participate in politics at least to the extent of voting. There is also a strong liberal community around Bloomington and the state university.

The strength of the parties, which are organized by elections from the ward level up, means that candidates chosen at the state convention will be backed by them in the general election. This changed in 1976 when Indiana, for the first time, held a statewide primary, but until then it enabled both parties to field unusually strong candidates who did not necessarily reflect the political biases within the state. Although there are always some tensions between a campaign organization and the party structure, the two organizations usually work well together because they avoid the sustained conflict that primaries often evoke.

The combination of demographic diversity and strong parties means that no candidate can expect to win by more than a few percentage points, and that consequently all elections are hotly contested, uncertain in their outcome, and marked by an unusual sophistication in campaign techniques. The Bayh campaign was clearly the most professional of the three studied, in the sense that tasks were well thought out, application was made of the latest techniques, and the staff had some distance from their campaign roles and the candidate.

This was Bayh's third election to the Senate, and the campaign reflected the past in its strategy and organizational priorities. Bayh was well known in the state; hence there was no need for billboards, newspaper advertising, or electronic media ads to get his name across. According to the polls, he had a 98 percent "name recognition factor," which meant that 98 percent of the voters at least knew who he was. He had a record in the Senate and he ran on it, structuring the campaign to focus on those issues that would appeal to the state's electorate. He used radio and television ads produced by the staff, but he did not buy either billboard or newspaper space.

The campaign was a mix of computer technology and grass roots organization. The technology enabled it to focus on issues, because the staff was able to gather information about those things that concerned the electorate through polls and an issue-identification program that used volunteers across the state. Computers also played a large role in fund raising, enabling the staff to assemble up-to-date lists of potential donors for a direct mail campaign.

The field operation was designed to do two things. The first was to promote the concept of a "friend talking to a friend," particularly through the use of a "note day program" in which volunteers were given packets of note paper, envelopes, and sample letters, and asked to write ten of their friends explaining why they were supporting Birch Bayh. This approach to campaigning moves away from reliance on impersonal paid media ads and is based on the awareness that voters are most likely to be swayed by informal opinion leaders in their circle of friends and associates. The second field operation objective was to identify and mobilize workers who would be able to register Democratic voters and get them out on election day — an especially important objective in a state based on ward politics.

The past was an important factor in helping the Bayh staff set priorities and establish the balance they wanted between technology and field work. It may well be that each race an incumbent runs is in large measure a compensation for the failings of the last race. The 1974 Bayh campaign staff paid constant attention to income and expenditures, partly because of the new federal campaign finance laws but also because the 1968 race had resulted in a debt of over $100,000, and the senator and his staff were determined to avoid that problem this time.

Another factor that caused the staff to focus so much of its energy on technology and field organization was the likelihood that the senator would have to spend most of his time in Washington during the height of the election season because of the impeachment trial of Richard Nixon. Although Bayh did eventually spend 175 days in the field (more than either Alexander or Sargent), the organization effort was almost strong enough to stand alone.

The average age of the Bayh campaign staff was comparable to the average of those working in the other campaigns. One difference, however, was that the campaign staff, which was largely drawn from the permanent Senate staff, had been with Bayh for a long time. David Bochnowski, the campaign field manager, was twenty-nine years old — the same age as the managers of the other two campaigns. Whereas Gary Sisco in Tennessee and Steve Crosby in Massachusetts had not worked extensively with the candidates before the campaigns, Bochnowski had been with Bayh for nine years.

Leadership in the Bayh organization came primarily from within, as people worked their way up after beginning as interns in college. (The two notable exceptions to that rule, whose connections with the Senator had evolved along other lines, had considerable difficulty being accepted by the staff, though this was partly due to their own efforts to upset the status quo in order to find places for themselves.) Having been together for a long time undoubtedly made it easier to assign tasks and responsibilities with confidence in the abilities of those charged with carrying them out, though such was not always the case. Communications problems did arise because the staff was so task oriented: people working in one area had little information about what others were doing. The problems were exacerbated by the physical arrangements of the campaign headquarters, which was housed in a building that had formerly been a car dealership. There were two large office areas divided by a cold dank garage that leaked when it rained. Those on one side of the garage were likely to get along better with their near neighbors than with those on the other side of the garage.

There were, of course, other problems in communication that arose in the Bayh campaign, one of which is particularly interesting because it is endemic to campaign organizations in general and Democratic campaigns in particular. The Democratic party is a coalition of clearly identifiable segments of the population. Campaign organizations tend to reflect the demographic composition of the party; hence there are people in the organization specifically charged with responsibility for these groups: labor, blacks, youth, and so on. During the study the black group was planning a fund raiser — a jazz concert to be held in Indianapolis — that they initially claimed would bring $85,000 in to the campaign coffers. The small group of blacks planning the concert worked on their own, partly because they wanted it to be a black affair (contributing so large a sum would raise their status within the organization) and partly because they had trouble communicating with the rest of the staff, particularly the finance department.

As the date for the concert drew near it became apparent there were going to be problems. Tickets were not selling as well as expected, and physical arrangements for the performers were becoming increasingly complicated. The blacks felt they were not being helped by the whites on the staff, and the whites were unsure of whether they could or should offer help. Although the problem was not racial in origin, it was complicated by the difficulties in communication that often occur across race lines in this country. Four days before the concert was scheduled to take place, a meeting was called by the campaign manager to decide whether to go ahead with it or to back out and lose the $15,000 in "front money" the campaign had already advanced.

For the blacks the meeting was rather a shock. They found it difficult to believe that anyone in the organization would be asking so late in the day whether or not to go ahead with the event. As one of them commented, "It was a typical campaign meeting when it comes to blacks. It was never considered by the campaign as a major fund raiser, especially by the press department." To the blacks the lack of attention, particularly by the press department, was a sign of their low standing in the organization. But to the whites in the organization, especially to the finance department (which had closer contact with the blacks because they were on the same side of the garage), the blacks appeared to want to go it alone. As one of the whites put it, "Initially they wanted their own show and their own thing, but they weren't able to bring it off. And now they complain about the lack of resources."

One of the white observers of the meeting and all that preceded it summed up the matter this way: "It was the fault of both sides. Lack of communication, and lack of organization. It was a power conflict between the whites who have the ability to do something, and the blacks who said they wanted to do their own thing. The blacks are trying to pull off something that the financial section usually pulls off. Finance is saying to them, 'You are doing my job. You are doing what I wanted to do. This is my job and what I normally do. No one else should be doing my job.' But the blacks had lived with this for so long they weren't looking at the finance end, they were doing a people thing."

In the end the concert did take place even though it lost money. A similar affair had a similar outcome in the Massachusetts campaign, but it was less important to the organization because the Sargent campaign was less financially oriented and because the staff working on the Massachusetts fund raiser was not a separate racial group. Excluding the power plays, which there were, and excluding the question of personal feelings, which were hurt by the process, the problem in Indiana was magnified by failures in interracial communication. As one of the finance people put it, "The highly compartmentalized nature of the campaign makes those in the organization not want to see a project fail, so they will go down to the wire on it. Perhaps that makes it even more difficult for the department head to be able to make a value judgment. It is a problem of balancing this one success against the total campaign good. Probably only the head of the organization can do that, but he doesn't have enough information to do it."

Another organizational problem that beset the Bayh campaign was less dramatic, but had greater significance for the permanent Senate staff and reflected a problem seen in all three campaigns. The issue was a question of efficiency: who was efficient, who was not, and why. Although the lines were drawn according to which side of the garage people worked on, the physical arrangements were only secondary causes. At the heart of the controversy was a man brought into the organization as the operations manager. He handled the books and the flow of work to the clerical support staff. A good friend of a longtime member of the staff, he was familiar with Bayh campaigns in the past, though this was his first experience in politics and he was using the experience to consider whether or not he would have a future in it.

The charge was made that the field organization staff, which worked on the other side of the garage, was inefficient. They did not work long enough or hard enough, and they did not know what they needed to get the job done in terms of such things as the numbers of pieces of literature. According to members of the field organization, they had trouble getting their letters typed and the literature they needed reproduced, and their work could not be measured by whether or not they were in the office at eight o'clock in the morning. Although it was the operations manager who spoke most openly about the competitive nature of the campaign organization and the "continual undercutting," he was also the one most often accused of undercutting others through his control of the work flow.

Unlike many of the tasks in a campaign, those under the supervision of the operations manager did lend themselves to some form of evaluation. As he put it, "There is a way to measure the manual tasks. We ought to let the dreamers dream and the machines run." Because it was a new environment for him, and because he was using the campaign experience to test his own potential in politics, the operations manager was very conscious of the difference between himself and others, particularly when it came to making decisions. As he put it, "If you are a legislator, you are not out front on the decision. The opposite 'business approach' is to make the decision and be right 60–70 percent of the time. The legislative way is to weigh the decision and come in at the last moment. One breeds efficiency and one breeds effectiveness. . . . We knew three weeks ago that we were going to do a mailing today. We didn't get to writing the thing until yesterday. We tend to say, 'Here's what I want run, but don't run it until I see what's in the papers tomorrow morning.' " (It is interesting to note that people in the gubernatorial races spoke of this quality of waiting until the last moment as an administrative decision-making style.)

The operations manager was apparently successful in his bid to undermine the confidence the candidate had in his field organization, until the question was raised as to whether or not efficiency was the primary objective of a political organization. As long as he could show others to be inefficient, the operations manager appeared to be in the ascendancy, partly because he also appealed to the strength of another relatively new member of the organization who had been a banker before he joined the staff. There was a bond of interest between those two, who had business backgrounds, as opposed to those who were "inefficient." The campaign organization was peculiarly subject to the charge of inefficiency because of the debt incurred in 1968. For the outsiders in an organization where the staff, although young, had many years of experience working together, playing on their own strengths and everyone else's apparent weakness may have been the only way they could become part of the organization: splitting it, and shattering the loyalties built up among the staff over the years.

The question of efficiency put a strain on the members of the organization. It reached a climax during the period of the study and then subsided as an issue when other pressures succeeded it. Throughout the period, however, decisions were made by those charged with responsibility for a task, and when there were differences of opinion, the final decision was made by the senator's administrative assistant or by the senator himself. Occasionally the staff were in agreement on something and were faced with the problem of convincing the candidate to go along. The years they had been together made it easier for them to know what Bayh would and would not accept, and how he and any dissident members of the staff might be influenced to change their minds.

Massachusetts

The campaign in Massachusetts was between Francis W. Sargent, the Republican incumbent governor, and Michael S.

Dukakis, the Democratic challenger. As a campaign organization, the Sargent race fell somewhere in between the highly professionalized Bayh organization and the personalized campaign of Alexander in Tennessee. Because Sargent was the incumbent governor, there were in fact two organizations: his personal staff, which worked at the statehouse and determined the strategies and tactics of the campaign; and the campaign organization, which was responsible for the field organization and the implementation of strategies developed at the statehouse. They were separate organizations, composed of people with very different backgrounds and styles of behavior. The statehouse group was more akin to the personalized campaign in that there was relatively little differentiation of tasks, and personalities played a primary role in decision making. Of the three campaigns, this group was also more representative of an older style of politics. Sargent's campaign organization, in contrast, was younger, somewhat differentiated in tasks (although much alike in background and personal style), and more organizationally conscious.

Massachusetts is a highly politicized state. Perhaps this is because of the large number of universities and young people in the Boston area, which comprises the bulk of the state's population, making it very much an urban state. Or perhaps, as *The Almanac of American Politics* suggests, it is because of the Yankee-Irish confrontation a century ago, which has led to a very active politics that has brought more people into the political system than is normally the case in America.[5] Whatever the reasons, the politicization of the state does not mean it is particularly partisan: evidence the ability of liberal Republicans to get elected (for example, Sargent, Edward Brooke, and Elliot Richardson) when their party has only 500,000 registered supporters. In contrast, there are 1,200,000 Democrats and 1,000,000 independents.

A large portion of the Sargent campaign staff knew the opposing candidate and his staff personally. Some had worked for or with Dukakis in the past. Partly because of their personal

---

[5]Michael Barone, Grant Ujifusa, and Douglas Matthews, *The Almanac of American Politics* (Cambridge: Grant, 1974), 434.

knowledge, and partly because both candidates were liberals, the Massachusetts race was marked by very little hostility to the opposition at the staff level. As many people on the staff noted, they were working for Sargent because they thought he would be the better governor, but it would not be the end of the world if Dukakis won the election. This rather sanguine attitude was in marked contrast to the other campaigns studied. On the other hand, because both sides had agreed to a series of televised debates, the Sargent campaign staff paid more attention to the substance of what the opponent said than did either of the campaigns in Tennessee and Indiana. The Sargent strategy sessions were more typical of what people expect campaigns to be all about: tactics designed to meet specific charges and to put the opposition on the defensive.

The campaign was studied during the last two weeks in October. There was no question that Sargent, as a Republican and an incumbent, was behind in the race, but there was a question as to how far behind he was and whether he would be able to pick up enough steam to overtake Dukakis. The uncertainty was compounded by differences shown in the polls. The campaign's own poll showed Sargent trailing by 10 points in mid-October; a poll published by the leading Boston newspaper showed him 25 points behind. If the newspaper was right there was probably little hope. If the campaign pollster was right, they stood a fighting chance. A good deal of time was devoted to trying to understand the differences and to respond.

Another factor that affected the campaign throughout the general election period was the relationship of the governor to the state Republican party. All three campaigns revealed some tensions between the campaign staffs and the party organizations, but in Massachusetts it was all-out war. Sargent's liberal positions as governor were taken because of the interests of his personal staff, most of whom were Democrats. He had done little over the years to build a close relationship with the various liberal constituencies in the state, and when he did go out to political affairs he went to the old Republican regulars.

By 1974, Sargent had alienated the party regulars on the issues, and he failed to replace that constituency with the liberals who might have supported him. The situation was complicated by the opposition Sargent had expressed to Richard Nixon in the early phase of the Watergate scandal. At the state Republican convention in the spring of 1974, Sargent was challenged for his lack of support of the party at the national and at the state level. Many of his appointments appeared to have gone to Democrats. Although he carried the convention there was a primary on September 10. The campaign strategy was to run against the party, with a slogan that said, "Frank Sargent doesn't dress for the Party." Geared to attract the attention of the state's Democratic and independent voters for the general election, the strategy was successful in garnering much of the media attention and in presenting Sargent as a fighter — a difficult image for an incumbent to maintain.

The primary strategy made it hard, however, to mobilize the party for the general election six weeks later. The campaign staff was also aware that their opponent had what was reputed to be the best organization Democrats had ever fielded. It took a while to sort out the strategy for the general election, perhaps complicated by what one aide suggested: that "the chief policy advisor has been trying to mold Frank Sargent into Mike Dukakis. After the primary he was faced with what he had been running for, and he didn't know what to do with Michael as an opponent. He didn't know how to fight that. How can you accuse him now when he was your role model?"

By the time of the study, the strategy was apparent: to challenge the credibility of Dukakis and his running mate, Thomas P. O'Neill, III, the son of the Speaker of the House. The attack was based on what appeared to be wavering statements made by the Democrats. There were also differences in personality stressed between the two gubernatorial candidates: Sargent open, friendly, with a sense of humor; and Dukakis closed, arrogant, incapable of recognizing a mistake. The tactics used to implement the strategy were tied to the televised debates that occurred each week (and press reactions to the debates), to the paid media advertising, and to the incursions the Sargent campaign was able to make into the liberal community, which appeared in the beginning to stand firmly behind the Dukakis candidacy.

There was some disagreement as to whether Sargent could

or should try to mount a strong field organization, and by the end of the campaign there was considerable disagreement about whether or not an effective field force had been created. The disagreement was largely between those working at the statehouse (who said a strong field force did not exist) and those in the campaign headquarters (who said either that it did, or else that it did not need to exist).

The Statehouse Staff

More than in either of the other two campaigns, the personalities in the Sargent organization had considerable impact on what people did and how they felt about it. This was particularly true at the statehouse. Sargent's administrative style was to make decisions by having people representing wide spectrums of opinion argue it out in the same room. As it turned out, by the fall of 1974 the two major protagonists represented different backgrounds and differed with each other considerably on style and attitude, but less so on the substance of issues.

Complicating the relationship between the two top aides, Jack Flannery (chief secretary) and Al Kramer (chief policy advisor), were stylistic differences that both described as irreconcilable. Flannery was time-conscious, concerned with details, and viewed himself as a reporter of opinions more than an advocate. Kramer was never on time and had what was described as a "high tolerance for ambiguity." He was creative and forceful in advocating ideas. Perhaps a deeper difference was what each of them thought was necessary for greatness: for Kramer it was the programmatic confrontation with the issues; for Flannery it was the romantic confrontation of the man and the events. The combination worked well when Flannery put Kramer's ideas into strong and dramatic speeches; it did not work when Flannery's reaction to Kramer would be to say, "It doesn't matter. It's not real. Forget about it — they're all clowns anyway."

The differences between Flannery and Kramer were played off against Sargent in a way that exaggerated or amplified their roles vis-à-vis each other. Flannery's provincial Irishness,

Kramer's "poor Jewish boy from Chelsea" image, and Sargent's patrician Waspishness represent the stereotypes that make up our political culture. All three played those stereotypes against each other — usually with great wit and considerable charm. Perhaps it would not have worked if there had not been such a balance.

Kramer and Flannery had been with Sargent longer than any other member of the staff. As one observer described it, "Sargent trusted them the most, and relied on them the most, despite the fact that they had totally different and strongly conflicting value systems. Al has the most creative, facile mind I've ever seen and an immensely healthy ego — one with self-imposed blind spots. He is driven by ego and guilt, with a strange interplay that can be noble. He loves to be persecuted and he takes things from Jack no one else would take. Very few other ideas are allowed to surface. He tends to ridicule people who disagree with him. He has an incredible verbal capacity and can paint the most convincing picture based on less fact than anyone else I've ever known. Jack, on the other hand, is openly disrespectful toward those who work hard. He doesn't encourage people to work hard and deceive themselves. The younger staff are loyal to Al and they don't like Jack. They don't respect his view of government and what it's all about. He is too casual and cynical. Al without Jack could survive. He couldn't run the office; there would have to be a check on him. But Jack would be lost without Al."

The relationship between Flannery and Kramer was deep, caring, and bitter at the same time, but also exclusive. While they may have been impatient with each other, they certainly were with others "who haven't been that route."[6] Kramer had a visible cadre of supporters; Flannery's supporters were less obvious, but just as caring about him. There did not appear to be any significant members of the staff who were not part of one side or the other in the struggle between the two top aides. One reason may have been the immense charm both of them had. Kramer's oft cited verbal capacity could weave

---

[6]Interview with Jack Flannery, Massachusetts chief secretary, October 21, 1974.

magic, and Flannery's private side was compelling and quite the opposite of the cynical public image. According to many, he also "knew the score politically."

There were other staff people who played important roles in the campaign, most notably the press secretary, Tom Reardon, who added stability to the group and was often the balance, or swing, influence in decision making. But on the whole the relationship between Kramer and Flannery defined the statehouse staff and reached out as well to those few members of the campaign staff who had any contact with the upper echelon. The struggle between Flannery and Kramer had lasted six years (as long as Sargent had been governor), and by the last two weeks in the 1974 campaign, both were tired and aware that the end was in sight for them whether or not Francis Sargent was re-elected. Several campaign aides felt that the battle was detrimental to the governor, and they tried to keep him out of the statehouse as much as possible. The fact that Sargent was the sitting governor in Massachusetts, and that Boston, the state's capital and largest city, was in the midst of the busing crisis, made it rather difficult.

The Campaign Staff

The statehouse is a landmark in Boston, with its golden dome reflecting from the top of Beacon Hill. Sargent's campaign headquarters was down the hill in an office building on Congress Street, about a ten-minute walk away. The campaign manager and the director of the field organization were the only members of the campaign staff who regularly attended meetings at the statehouse. For the rest of the staff — with the exception of those who had worked in state government before — there was curiosity about the statehouse group, but only a low level of awareness of who the people were and what roles they played in the campaign. Both Al Kramer and Jack Flannery could have walked through the headquarters unrecognized.

The campaign headquarters had its own tensions and divisions, most notably between the field staff and the rest of the organization, many of whom formed a group of their own because they had worked together on a congressional campaign two years before. The tension between the two groups was exacerbated by the physical arrangements, with the field staff in a large open room of their own. But there were probably deeper reasons for the antagonism and sense of isolation felt between the two sides. Steve Crosby, the campaign manager, was very conscious of organization dynamics and inclined to be inclusive in his decision-making style. Most of those who did not identify with the field staff had worked with him in the past and admired and expected that style of behavior. The head of the field organization, William Najam, and his deputy, James Velis, came from the state government and had a bureaucratic style of decision making: centralized and hierarchical, with limited access to information. Their department had more support staff than any other seen in the study. Beside the director and his deputy, it included a co-director (who actually did more work with the party and special projects, and appeared to operate independently), six in-house advisors (the professional staff charged with responsibility for the state's fourteen counties), four secretaries, several assistants, a driver, and someone who handled the distribution of materials.

In contrast to the field organization staff in Indiana, the Massachusetts staff came in early, stayed late, and questioned the efficiency of the rest of the organization. One member of the field staff described their sense of solidarity this way: "We are close together, though the work is usually fragmented into different areas. But in the field office the spirit is closer than with us and the rest of the staff. There is a physical separation of the office which sets a bit of the tone. We are doing a specific thing, our priorities are different, the way we go about it — our outlook is different." Another member of the field staff put it more graphically: "There are blockheads here, but not in the field staff." From the other side came this view: "Steve's staff and the people he hired and Najam's staff and the people he hired have split the campaign down the middle. The people Bill hired are not as neat, well-rounded, or intelligent as the people Steve hired. He puts pressure on his people by saying, 'if you don't shape up, you are not going to get a job in November.' Steve gives people a task and checks back with them. Most of his people are working for him and for the governor . . . more of it is for him. Najam is not particularly creative, he's more of a nuts and bolts kind of guy. Steve is more of a creative guy, but also good on follow-through. Najam yells at people and says that the most effective way to get something done is to be firm." Perhaps it could all be summed up by the comments of another disenchanted observer: "I have never seen a campaign that is as divided between the personalities and philosophies of major objectives and end results. An end result to Bill can be a list of names, whereas to Steve, the end result is a hundred votes." The same could be said for the statehouse organization.

The problem of the relationship between the field staff and the rest of the campaign organization existed throughout the campaign. In the last week, a new problem arose between the campaign headquarters and the statehouse group. Until then, contact between the two organizations had been minimal, but as the campaign came to a close and the policy work at the statehouse ended, the focus of the campaign shifted from concentrating on the debates to the question of whether or not the field organization was effective. The solution, according to Al Kramer, was to bolster the field staff by sending down members of the statehouse staff, who would take a leave of absence or vacation time to volunteer.

On the one hand, it is a fairly typical campaign phenomenon that the closer an election gets, the less there is to do (particularly for those who have been working on policy). On the other hand, there is a growing sense of anxiety — fed by the running out of time and the running out of things to occupy the mind, by the narrowing of options and the increasing irrelevance of everything that will not lead to the ultimate objective of winning the election. It was not surprising, therefore, that Kramer felt the need to supplement the headquarters staff with his own aides. At the same time, however, the headquarters staff was reaching the climax of all its work; their sense of group solidarity had been strengthened not only by the time and experience members of the group shared, but also by the knowledge that the experience was soon to end. Intrusion by the statehouse group was threatening to their organizational solidarity, and, not surprisingly, it was rebuffed.

After several communications failures, a week before the election a meeting was held between members of both organizations. From the perspective of the headquarters staff, the statehouse group appeared to be offering to take over a major role — such as get-out-the-vote activity on election day — with the underlying assumptions that the field organization was a failure and that the campaign staff was jealous of the statehouse staff. Consequently the former did not treat the latter very well. From the statehouse perspective, the campaign organization was, at best, resentful and, at worst, fearful that the people on the governor's staff would discover that there was no field operation after all. As one member of the statehouse staff put it, "These people at Congress Street already see a full staff here, so they would have to come in over our bodies. I imagine there's a lot of frustration down there toward us." Another described it this way: "I was prepared to go down there, but not to go down there and have nothing to do — which has become the greatest complaint of everyone, including the secretaries. I see that organization as inefficient. Also, they don't like our people. They are more conservative and party oriented; here people are all Democrats and very proud of working for Frank Sargent. The people down there are not even political pragmatists, they are living in never-never land. But you don't do anything that you don't like. We were constantly told that the people down there were keeping a list of who was working and who would get a job after the election."

It was not only organizational integrity that was at stake when the attempt was made (however superficially) to merge the two groups, but also very real political and personal differences, which made the attempt frustrating for both sides. One person succeeded in making the transition and her reactions are particularly illuminating:

> The cause of the failure was that people felt that it wasn't exciting enough for them down there [campaign headquarters] — making calls was a dull, boring thing. Also, from the start we saw a lot of resentment up here [statehouse] about going down to help out. Some did it, but others felt they were already doing the job they were paid for and it was too much to ask of them. Others felt we were going to lose and what they did was not going to make a

difference and their time was more valuably spent in other things. What we were doing up here was, for the majority of offices, campaign-oriented. Some of the feedback that I heard up here (and felt myself before the last week) was that you went down there and the staff wasn't friendly and didn't try to get to know you. I felt rebuffed when I made a few suggestions about stuffing envelopes. Maybe if they had been a little more discriminating in what they brought us down there to do. A lot of time they were really very mechanical things they wanted people to do — and people felt it was really a drag. People up here were really picky about what they would and would not do: they didn't want to make phone calls, or do standouts with signs on the bridges. They were very absolute in what they didn't want to do. They said they would do anything but make phone calls, but they wouldn't.

I knew very few of the people when I went down there for the last week, but from the very first day I got there everyone went out of their way to get to know me and offer whatever help they could. It was great to get away from that negative attitude. It was a delightful surprise. It turned out to be a great experience and once I got down there I was very impatient with the people up here. I felt that good people had misled me and they should have said forthrightly that they didn't want to go down there. I became somewhat resentful toward those people.

I had the impression — all of us up here felt that we were doing the substantial work of the campaign: doing the speeches, press releases, research on the issues — and we felt we were more important than the campaign staff. When I got down there, I got the opposite view: that they were doing the important things, and the people in the statehouse weren't doing anything but sitting around all day. I knew at least this part of the statehouse staff was busy, but maybe the other people weren't.

I was amazed when I got down there. I couldn't imagine what else they were doing beside stuffing envelopes because it seemed we were doing everything else. I had heard comments up here that if we win this, it will be because of what we're doing up here, not because of the campaign organization. Everything was blamed on them.[7]

Partly because the policy decisions were made at the statehouse, Steve Crosby had placed special emphasis on

[7]Interview with Barbara Tapley, Massachusetts statehouse staff member, November 14, 1974.

building organizational solidarity by having everyone share in such mechanical tasks as stuffing envelopes or handing out literature on the sidewalk on special days. If the statehouse group saw the campaign staff as being excessively occupied with mechanical tasks, or if they felt they were being asked to perform tasks beneath their status, it was more likely due to the difference in organizational style than to any intent to demean the statehouse volunteers.

Because Sargent was the incumbent governor, it was necessary that he have two organizations. The situation was unlike the incumbency of Birch Bayh, whose permanent staff lived and worked in Washington, D.C., and whose campaign staff functioned as a single organization because even those who came from Washington did not travel back and forth. The problem was to blend the work, and it was the consensus of opinion in both groups that an overall manager could have done it. Given the personalities involved, there was no likelihood of any of them performing the managerial role, partly because Jack Flannery, the logical choice, had seen his predecessor wear himself thin in that capacity and did not want the task, and partly because any organization would have been hard pressed to cope with the creativity of Al Kramer, who began every day with another new idea.

These were the details of the three campaigns. There are generalizations to be drawn about the people who participated in them. Although none of those studied knew members of campaigns in other states, they all shared some common experiences and they held some common expectations about themselves and the campaigns in which they worked. The commonalities are the subject of the next chapter.

Chapter 3

The People Who Work in Campaigns

The people who worked in the 1974 campaigns were a new generation of political actors. They were different from the oldtime regulars — the "pols" and "hacks" of the days of ward politics, and they were different from the liberal reformers of the 1950s and 1960s — the "amateurs," described by James Q. Wilson, who brought a sense of righteousness into politics.[1] As a new generation, they combined some of the characteristics of their predecessors and some of the characteristics of their contemporaries who are not necessarily part of the traditional political world. To a large extent they were — like any new generation — in reaction against the past.

Much of what is distinctive about them depends on age: when they "came of age" politically, and where they are in the

---

[1] James Q. Wilson, *The Amateur Democrat* (New York: Basic Books, 1974).

life cycle.[2] Some of the difference depends upon the degree of commitment to the organization: people on the periphery of the organization can be explained by variables different from those used in understanding the behavior of people centrally involved.

There are two major categories of participants in the campaigns: those who participated as a *vocation,* and those who did so as an *avocation.*[3] The significance of the distinction is that for those whose work is a full-time vocation, the initial motivation is irrelevant in explaining their actions in the organization. Those for whom politics is an avocation are often volunteers on the periphery of the organization — either in the campaign headquarters or in the field — and their motivation explains much of their behavior. They are not so engaged by the dynamics of the organization as to blur or change their response to the campaign's incentives. Being farther away from the center of things, they tend to have an exaggerated idea of what politics is and to be guided by their perceptions of "the rules of the game."

In the vocational category there are the *organizers,* who are the largest and most politically significant group; the *apprentices,* who are younger and far fewer in number; and the *seekers,* who are older than the organizers and are using the campaign as a platform from which to consider the prospects of a new life for themselves. Among the avocational participants are the *believers,* those for whom the purposive incentive of civic-mindedness is a reward in itself; the *materialists,* who

---

[2]Sidney Verba and Norman H. Nie, *Participation in American Political Democracy and Social Equality* (New York: Harper and Row, 1972), 138–148. (New York: Basic Books, 1974).

[3]Weber describes the vocationalist this way: "He who lives 'for' politics makes politics his life in an internal sense. Either he enjoys the naked possession of political power he exerts, or he nurses his inner balance and self-feeling by the consciousness that his life has *meaning* in the service of a 'cause'." He describes the avocationalist as someone who "may engage in politics, and hence seek to influence the distribution of power within and between political structures, as an 'occasional politician' . . . . Politics as an avocation is today practiced by all those party agents and heads of voluntary political associations who, as a rule, are politically active only in case of need and for whom politics is, neither materially nor ideally, 'their life' in the first place." H. H. Gerth and C. Wright Mills, eds., From *Max Weber: Essays in Sociology* (New York: Oxford University Press, 1945), 83–84.

participate on a quid pro quo basis, wanting and expecting a reward for any service they provide the campaign; and the *joiners*, who respond to solidary incentives, participating because they want to meet people and because they enjoy the camaraderie campaigns provide.

In addition to the categories I have described, there were a few individuals who fit the descriptions of older political actors — reformers and regulars — which is not surprising, if one can assume some continuity in the political system. There were also some people for whom the campaign was a job like any other job; they were largely found in clerical roles.

The Vocationalists

The Organizers

The organizer views himself or herself as a political worker, at least for a few years. As a worker, the organizer expects to participate on a paid basis in several campaigns and to serve on the staffs of elected or appointed officials as an aide or in a line position. The commitment the organizer makes is to the political process, and the candidate is a vehicle for that commitment. It is not an intense personal commitment to the candidate. The organizer is "credentialed" by experience, rather than by a university or board of peers as a professional person might be.

There are two factors that distinguish the organizers: *situation*, that is, marital status and educational background; and *style*, the result of social and political circumstances. Both factors are dependent on age. Butler and Stokes, in *Political Change in Britain*, make the point that the "relative impressionability of the young . . . means they will be unusually open to the influence of issues and events which dominate national politics at the time of their entry into the electorate."[4] When they are a certain age is as important as what that age means in the life cycle.

The average age of the people I am describing as organizers

---

[4]David Butler and Donald Stokes, *Political Change in Britain* (New York: St. Martin's Press, 1971), 39.

is twenty-eight, which means they probably came of age politically with the experience of President Kennedy's assassination. It was their peers who participated in the civil rights movement and particularly in the peace movement of the middle and late 1960s. They were in school, or not long out of school, when the uprisings occurred in the universities in the latter part of the 1960s and the beginning of the 1970s.

Although some of them had been active participants in those social movements, most did not mention any such activity as a motive for current involvement. A surprising number of the Democrats said they chose a political career because they had been touched by Robert Kennedy, a man known for his pragmatism, his commitment to the system, and in the end, his care for the disestablished. His assassination was a particularly traumatic event for several of them. It may be that emotional commitments were made once or twice to political figures, but having been disappointed, these young people would not let themselves again make that kind of commitment to a charismatic leader.

The attitude the organizers held toward their candidates, their party, and the political system as a whole may well be the product of cumulative political history in America since their political awakening. Their lack of participation in the movements, as well as the scarcity of Democrats who described themselves as having come into the party because of Eugene McCarthy (compared to those who were motivated by Kennedy), suggests that while other members of their generation were making conscious choices to seek change outside the traditional political system, these people opted for change within it. Many of the young (and some of the old) people in the 1960s felt they had to take a stand that would define them as being on the right or the left. Those who did not take so definite a stand, or who decided not to be limited by favoring all the positions of the "side" they initially chose, may be the group from which the campaign organizers came. It may be that those who chose to work for change within the system (which would not be approved of by either side: the left denying the system; the right denying change), would tend to focus on process rather than substance, on the tasks of campaigning rather than the purity of working for an issue or a cause.[5]

Whatever the earlier experiences of the organizers in the 1974 campaign season, there was another historical tradition to which they were heir: the focus that presidential politics brings to campaigning. For those in the Democratic party, the cumulative political history went back at least as far as 1968, a year of tremendous emotional commitment on all sides. For the people who staff campaigns, 1972 was a year of "backing away"; they neither hated other candidates nor loved their own so much as they had four years before. The Kennedy people and the Humphrey people had gone to work for other candidates; the McCarthy supporters seemed to have disappeared, and were few and far between by the time of the 1974 season. For those in the Republican party, the Watergate scandal had been a heartrending experience. If less traumatic than assassination, it was equivalent at least in the sense of loss and in the uncertainty it generated for future commitments.

The organizers lacked any clear ideological orientation. Politically they tended toward the middle, varying slightly to the left or the right according to the circumstances of the campaign. In Tennessee, where the staff was carefully selected by Lamar Alexander to reflect his views, they tended to reflect also the views of the rest of the population in the state. In Indiana, which quite frequently elects statewide candidates who are

---

[5]This suggestion differs from the work of James M. Fendrich and Alison T. Tarleau in a 1973 article, "Marching to a Different Drummer: Occupational and Political Correlates of Former Student Activists," *Social Forces*, vol. 52 (Dec. 1973), 245–253. According to their study of civil rights demonstrators at Florida State University, political activists were more likely to be participants in party politics than those who participated in student government, or than a third group drawn from a cross section of the student population. The difference between their data and my own may be due to differences between the generations, which they, too, point to as a significant factor in political participation. Political activism off campus may not be nearly as psychologically significant as political activism on campus, which forces members of the university community to take a stand. It is also true that by the late 1960s and early 1970s, people had grown accustomed to confrontation politics as a style, and those who joined movements had a fairly clear idea of what that style would mean for themselves and for the institutions they sought to change — a clearer idea, perhaps, than those who pioneered the style in the civil rights movement.

more liberal than the state as a whole, the staff reflected the liberal orientation of Birch Bayh more than it did the state's population. And in Massachusetts, which is a more liberal state than most, the campaign staff reflected the bias of the slightly more conservative Republican party more than the bias of Francis Sargent and his personal staff.

Although there were occasionally people on the campaign staffs who were more ideologically conscious than most of their colleagues, they were generally to be found performing tasks that lent themselves to an ideological or issue orientation, such as research or organizing special constituencies.

Perhaps another reason why the 1974 campaign organizers appeared to be free of the kind of emotional commitment that characterized the 1960s was that they had grown accustomed to the idea of going from one campaign to another (though few had actually worked in more than two campaigns). Professionalism, in the sense of distance, can come from mobility or the expectation of mobility. In any case, the people who dominated the 1974 campaigns were fairly "cool" in their commitment and in their style of behavior. As one of them described it, "It's not as black and white as it used to be in the old days." In contrast to their predecessors in the 1950s and 1960s, they were not crusading against the enemy — they were working for the candidate and for the party. They were not issue oriented or caught up in ideology. They did not seek to sway opinion by demonstrations of forensic ability. Instead they had an inclusive decision-making style that was responsive to group sensibilities and was probably affected by the demands for participatory democracy so common to the earlier social movements. They were not as elitist as the liberal (or "amateur") reformers had been.

In contrast to the older political vocationalists — the regulars, the "pols" and "hacks" against whom the reformers mounted their cause — the organizers were relatively open in their decision-making style. They were not idealists who would never compromise their cause, but neither were they the wheelers and dealers of the old school. Underlying their pragmatism was a moral conviction about the political process, which grew out of the 1960s. Perhaps the most significant difference between the organizers and the regulars was the greater sense of personal efficacy the former brought to their role, doubtless a consequence of their higher educational attainments. Campaign participation, to the organizers, was not a necessary condition for being able to share in the distribution of power and material benefits that belong to the victor.

The organizers were also less power oriented than their predecessors had been. Power for the regulars was a measure of position in the political hierarchy, made visible in the ability to do favors for friends and constituents. Power for the reformers was a measure of the ability to bring about changes on social issues. For both, power was an end as well as a means. The organizers, in contrast, did not appear to have a serious power orientation, primarily, I think, because they were not measuring themselves against each other so much as their predecessors had. They were group oriented, which meant they did not have a strong sense of personal identification with their tasks or their role in the campaign. The task orientation in the context of an organizational environment meant that they placed themselves at a distance from their activities in a way that fits traditional definitions of professionalism. They measured their activities by objective standards: for example, how many pieces of literature they were able to distribute compared to their peers, to other parts of the organization, and to other campaigns. By seeking activities that could be measured by others as well as themselves, they demystified the process and lessened the identification of the individual with the task.

Out of a sample of 65 organizers, 62 percent were single, 84 percent were college graduates, and 17 percent held advanced degrees. This high percentage of well-educated people, unencumbered in terms of family responsibilities, certainly differentiates them from the population at large in their age group and probably differentiates them from the reformers and regulars as well. One major consequence of these characteristics was that strong sense of personal efficacy. They believed in their ability to succeed, and their horizons were quite broad — free, as they were, from the responsibilities that raising a family usually brings. Many of them worked in campaigns because they wanted tough, challenging jobs, not because they felt they had to pay their dues in order to be rewarded by those higher up in the political structure.

Another possibility — though whether it is cause or effect is not clear — is that the campaign experience fulfilled whatever needs the organizers had for a family life, for people with whom to share both professional and social activities. The intensity of the campaign experience was all-encompassing. As one organizer described it, "I can't wait to get out the door at night, but I am lonely at home."

Campaigns have always been all-consuming activities, but not being torn by competing responsibilities may have enabled the organizers to be absorbed more with less emotional strain. If emotional conflict heightens the intensity of one's activities, it may be that minimizing the strain also minimizes the need to seek personal rewards (or justifications) from the activity. In other words, the organizers did not need to amplify the importance of their individual participation in the campaign in order to compensate for guilt felt from failing to meet private responsibilities.

Another consequence of their situational characteristics was that the organizers were relatively mobile, and the campaign experience was less dislocating for them than it was for their predecessors. A number either had just completed their education or were considering returning to school. Any job would have been considered a temporary activity, and many of them said they could afford to give the time now because they were young and did not yet have to make commitments to a permanent career. "Young" is always a relative term, but to this group it meant being under thirty-five. It is quite probable that "young" to their predecessors meant being under twenty-one; perhaps an even younger limit would have been applied by the older regulars.

The prolonging of youth was a factor in the social dynamics of the 1960s.[6] Many complained that the war, which encouraged those who could to stay in school lest they be drafted, extended adolescence beyond a reasonable limit, and the de-

---

[6]Kenneth Kenniston, "Social Change and Youth in America," in Erik H. Erikson, ed., *The Challenge of Youth* (New York: Doubleday Anchor Books, 1965), 191–222.

mands by students for greater responsibility in determining their lives in the late 1960s resulted from keeping them in school too long. Whether that generation sought responsibility or avoided it, the expectation was nonetheless established that settling down was to be deferred until a much later time. The campaign organizers reflected that expectation and were, therefore, accustomed to mobility, to the dislocation in their private lives that mobility produces, and to the deferment of both career responsibilities and personal commitments. Perhaps that was another reason for the lack of a strong personal identification with what they were doing and the consequent lack of a power orientation.

There appear to be two clear consequences for the political system as a whole in the coming of age of the organizers: the deteriorating relationship between campaign organizations and party structures, and the shying away from charisma as a necessary attribute of the candidate. There has been a lot of speculation about the future of the Democratic and Republican parties, much of it having to do with declining voter identification with the parties. The increase in primaries and a number of other institutional changes were the outcome of the battle between the reformers and the oldtime regulars, victory going most often to the reformers.

Compared to their immediate predecessors, the organizers are much more organizationally minded and inclined to be concerned about the fate of the party. But they are, on the average, thirty years younger than the party regulars, and although they are eager for communication or coalition, it is difficult to attain. Even if the reformers had never existed as a generation in politics, there would still be a communications gap between the regulars and the organizers caused by age alone. But just as the characteristics of the organizer can be understood as the outcome of the cumulative experience of their politically conscious years, so too can the reaction of the regulars to the organizers be described as the outcome of their cumulative experience with new people coming into or opposing the system. If the regulars had learned to distrust the reformers, there was certainly nothing to encourage them about the organizers. The farther away one is from any group, the more members of that group tend to appear alike. It was very difficult for the regulars to distinguish the organizers from the radical activists who had appeared so dominant in their age group five years before. As one observer in Massachusetts described it, the relationship between the campaign organization and the party was compounded by the youth and inexperience of the staff: "They had no one who knew the names and numbers of the old players. It was a kiddy corps — good kids — but they didn't have anyone who was either heavy enough or respectable enough for the old pros."

The second consequence of the coming of age of the organizers is more psychological. Charisma is defined by Weber as "an *extraordinary* quality of a person, regardless of whether this quality is actual, alleged, or presumed . . . [which refers] to a rule over men, . . . to which the governed submit because of their belief in the extraordinary quality of the specific *person*."[7] Charisma implies a relationship between the actor and the audience. It is, therefore, something to be seen or looked for in the eyes of the beholders. It has been described as "voyeuristic," enabling the observer to witness the "unfolding of a personality," which permits both "the performer and the audience to relax their defences, to 'suspend disbelief' and to allow their emotions to surge and to join with those of others."[8]

The 1960s were "hot" political years, times that called for the suspension of disbelief, times that were made for and by charismatic leadership. They were costly years as well. The emotional commitments made by some political actors to others were destroyed by assassination or disappointment. The same could be said for the emotional commitments that were made to the causes of the 1960s.

Although charisma in political figures probably requires some distance, there must be a relationship between what is

---

[7]*Max Weber: Essays in Sociology*, 295.

[8]Abraham Zaleznik, "Charismatic and Consensus Leaders: A Psychological Comparison," in *Bulletin of the Menninger Clinic*, vol. 38, no. 3 (May 1974), 235.

felt by the voting population at large and what is felt by those who work with that leader on a day-to-day basis. It has something to do with the interaction of that individual and those around him, perhaps requiring their aid to maintain the myth. Governor Sargent was the most charismatic figure of the three candidates, and he was so perceived and treated by his immediate staff — a staff that was representative of an older political style. Senator Bayh, in contrast to Sargent, did not encourage special treatment or strong emotional commitments. He said they made him uneasy. He spoke of the first time he ran for the Senate and how strange it made him feel with himself. "The whole system is designed for a special this and a special that, especially when an incumbent has been around awhile. It's not healthy to be surrounded by people like that."[9] Lamar Alexander was not an incumbent, and therefore did not have that specialness which identification with the office can bring, as Bayh described it. It was also true that of all the candidates in the study, Alexander was the least flamboyant in personal style and the most representative of the new breed of organizers.

All three campaign staffs were low keyed in their personal style. Nowhere is this better seen than among the staff in Indiana, since as an incumbent Bayh had the potential of drawing on charisma, or, as he called it, a sense of "specialness," and he clearly did not want to. According to several members of his staff, Birch Bayh had the image of the "boy next door, a boy who made good in the eyes of Indiana voters." One staff member described him this way: "Senator Bayh does not encourage intense involvement. He is sort of detached." Another said of him, "We know the limits of Birch Bayh — the time limits — and what he's going to say when you ask him a question. We're pretty realistic about him."

The Indiana staff shied away from emotional commitment to the candidate partly because the candidate wanted them to and partly because they were not inclined to be caught up in charismatic commitment. One staff member spoke of the danger of "living vicariously — being a parasite on Birch Bayh's name. There is some sort of gratification in it, but I'm not sure

---

[9]Interview with Birch Bayh, October 10, 1974.

I'm being responsible to myself." The commitment to the campaign was total, but limited in time in the minds of most of the organizers. The limitation was a defense against the loss of their own identity, which might be acceptable at a certain age for a certain length of time but would ultimately be damaging to people with the strong sense of personal efficacy common to the organizers.

Another member of the Bayh staff summarized it this way: "The higher up you are — whether you are close to the candidate or not — the kinds of things that are required of you in a campaign — the job responsibilities and tasks are such as to minimize the emotional and ideological commitment. Whereas the farther away you are in your functional links to the campaign, the more likely you are to rely on a personal identity with the candidate. There are very complex human psychological factors involved: ego gratification, a sense of assurance, the need for some personal kind of relationship."

The Apprentices

The apprentices were college students on leave for the semester to participate in the campaign. They could be defined by their youth and their status as learners in the organization. They did not hold positions of responsibility and they were conscious of their lower status and lack of involvement in decision making. Their sense of being outside the inner group helped them learn because they observed others and found satisfaction in their role as observers.

The number of apprentices in the campaigns was small — for reasons that will become apparent — and most of them were found in the Bayh organization. They were usually interns on his staff in Washington, attending school at one of the Washington-based universities. Because college is a finite but rather full experience, they felt the pain of being away from "home" more than their elders did. As one of them described it, "Other people are used to having a nine-to-five job, and the campaign is just an extension of that job, but what I dislike is that I consider myself a little too young to put myself through this total dedication of my body and my life and my mind. It makes me realize how lucky I am now to have time for myself and my friends. It's hard to be away, but you have to think more of the future than of the present."

Given the fact that most of the organizers did not have families, or live in circumstances that tended toward close social relationships away from the job, the "hardship" of campaigning in terms of that loss was relatively negligible for them. On the other hand, to the apprentices, the temporary nature of college life made such relationships all the more precious, even more than family responsibilities might be for others.

Another difference between the organizers and the apprentices was the role each played in the campaign and the rewards those roles provided. Campaigns are task-oriented organizations, which is to say that there are very specific activities each campaign will undertake, most of which can be broken down into distinct and measurable parts: registering new voters, distributing literature, establishing committees of supporters, and so on. Many of the organizers spoke of their attraction to the campaign because of the responsibility they were given to perform those tasks. The apprentices, who worked as assistants to the organizers, had neither the responsibility nor the rewards that went with the responsibility. Since most of the tasks a campaign performs are routine in nature, the work of the apprentices was more drudgery than not. The apprentices did such things as assist the scheduler, help with literature distribution, handle minor research, and run the switchboard. Female apprentices were more likely to be found in traditional clerical roles than the male apprentices.

Adding to their sense of frustration was the isolation the apprentices felt from other activities in the campaign — particularly frustrating when they wanted to use their time as a learning experience and were involved more in a task-oriented campaign, with its narrower flow of information.

Because the apprentices were younger than the organizers, particularly in an incumbent's campaign, they felt they were not taken seriously. As one put it, "I am always reminded that I am an intern and younger, and what could I know?" Another noted that a lot of information was kept from them and that they had to check everything with their superiors, adding to their sense of being young and inexperienced.

Perhaps the most difficult thing for the apprentices was being subject to campaign tensions. All organizations have tensions, and they may or may not be greater in campaigns, but while the organizers tried to keep the frustrations within bounds when they dealt with each other, they were less sensitive to the feelings of the younger members of the staff who worked for others in the organization. At the same time, the apprentices were very much aware of the tensions provoked by others in their superiors and they tended to be protective of their seniors. Having less contact with other senior members of the organization, they had fewer opportunities to develop positive attitudes toward their organizational opponents and were, therefore, more set in opposition than their superiors were.

The apprentices were clearly interested in politics as a career, and in the Bayh case it was a serious enough interest for them to choose a school in Washington in the first place. Most of the Bayh staff had come up through the organization via the intern route, and that undoubtedly helped the apprentices by providing models for them of political roles they might themselves play some day.

The Seekers

Seekers were older members of the campaign organization (varying in age from mid-thirties to early fifties) who used the campaign as a forum from which to re-evaluate their professional careers. They shared a past that included family and career responsibilities, and their political activity was a change from their everyday lives. Several of them had been successful in business and were looking for something more out of life. One had had a severe shock when his partner committed suicide, and as he described it, his "primary motive for participation was self-protection against whatever caused my partner to go off the edge." The seekers were looking for new lives for themselves, possibly in politics, though not necessarily so.

Most of the seekers had participated in politics before as avocationalists, which is to say on an intermittent basis, that either did not take them away from other responsibilities or had occurred before they acquired them. Because they had experience, and particularly because they usually knew people around the state, the seekers held responsible positions in the campaigns, but they were not in key positions. In no case were they part of the inner group in a campaign.

It seems almost paradoxical to describe a campaign as a refuge, but it was just that for the seekers, and perhaps for the organizers as well. Of the three groups, the apprentices were the only ones obviously unhappy about being taken away from their everyday lives. A campaign can be a refuge because it is a serious all-consuming endeavor. Although it may provide an important professional return should the candidate become governor and appoint his staff to state posts, or should the candidate be elected to the Senate and recommend his supporters for federal positions, there are no guarantees this will be so. The possibility of holding office was important to the seeker, but more as a way to justify his or her activity to family and friends than anything else, I suspect. As one person described it, "Honey, I'm as high as I want to go, and sometimes I think I am higher than I wish I was." The seekers sought refuge from which to consider change; they were not seeking commitments for change.

Another reward seekers suggested was available to them (though again not a necessary incentive) was the possibility of influence, described by one person as follows: "The rewards in a senatorial campaign are really intangible. In a governor's campaign you have patronage available to you. It's sort of against the law, but everyone knows that it's there at the end of the road. With a senator, you are thinking about national and international policies, and that's pretty intangible. Many people work here not because they want a job, but because they have a friend who wants a job. What they want is influence that they can exert. Being able to do favors is a yardstick that people outside politics can apply. I have three friends who don't think I have any clout at all because I don't get their speeding tickets fixed."

The influence, the potential for future jobs, and the extended contacts are the justifications seekers express for taking time away from other responsibilities. Of all the people who work in campaigns, the seekers probably have the greatest number of outsiders watching them: families, longtime friends, neighbors, and business associates. They may, therefore, have the greatest need to justify their activity. The organizers, in contrast, are relative loners, and the apprentices come from a world that is completely in transition.

The Avocationalists

The Believers

We are taught in school that a democracy is dependent upon its citizenry to share the burdens of public responsibility. For most people, most of the time, there is little opportunity to share any responsibility. We tend to judge the relevance or success of the system of government by the proportion of the potential electorate who vote. Those who assume a greater burden of the public responsibility are the political elite, and they are a very small portion of the population. Many people, in both the vocational and avocational categories, derive satisfaction from fulfilling their civic responsibilities and being part of that elite, but for the believers that is their primary incentive and only reward. As one of them described it, "I like the opportunity to get involved and to feel that you are helping a candidate whose philosophy is like your own. . . . A lot of people work in [politics] for ideological reasons, rather than for the monetary or personal gains. The volunteers give a lot of time, but they don't get very much in return. They never see the campaign manager or the candidate."

The believers held traditional values. They believed in the system and they felt good about meeting their civic responsibilities, even if they did not "get very much in return." As another described it, "Everyone should participate. It is a birthright to believe in the person who would do the best job and to get out and work for him."

Most of the believers were women with an average age of fifty-one. Sex and age account in large measure for the traditional nature of their views and the lack of expectation of a more tangible reward for their services. Again, it is a question of where they are in the life cycle, and what expectations they held when they came of age politically. These women lived traditional lives: they were married and had children, but their children were grown and they needed something else to fill their days. Their educational backgrounds varied, though six of the eight women who fit into this category had not gone further than high school. Their education and the social values dominant in their youth were critical factors in their attitudes toward the campaign. They believed in the political process and their civic responsibility to help that process along. They did not expect a return for themselves because women of their age and backgrounds were expected to perform support rather than leadership functions. Their perceptions of the campaign were based on texbook notions of civic duty and hence (unlike what one would have predicted) they were more drawn by purposive incentives than the upper-middle-class professionals. But the sense of purpose was not an ideology; it was too primitive and superficial.

The work the believers performed were the routine tasks that are normally assigned to volunteers: collating papers, making telephone calls, typing, and stuffing envelopes.

The Materialists

Whereas the believers acted upon a conception of what ought to be, the materialists viewed the political world in terms of the distribution of goods and services, which had exact measures available for all the world to see. For the most part, the materialists were found among the men who made up the volunteer field organizations in the campaigns. Sometimes they were identified with the party structure, sometimes they were part of a parallel structure, and sometimes they were not part of any structure and had only incidental contacts with the campaign. Because their participation in the campaign was entirely within their local community, they were much more responsive to the concrete measures of their influence, such as a low-number license plate or the ability to appoint their friends and supporters to office.

For the materialists there were two possible rewards: a job or prestige, which meant being identified as a source of power.

Both rewards are more obvious at the local level than at the campaign level because everyone within the campaign organization has a job and has some measure of influence. It is out in the field that political people are watched and evaluated as if they lived in a fishbowl. I would imagine that whereas 90 percent of the friends and associates of the campaign vocationalists were in politics, the opposite would be true at the county or town level. Because we apply something of a double standard to our politicians (assuming they are up to some nefarious or self-rewarding activity on the one hand, and on the other making them very popular at parties because they are, after all, "in the know" about what is going on), those who do participate at the local level may require more specific rewards to justify their activities and assure their positions in the political hierarchy. As one observer in Tennessee noted, "Everyone wants to be the first person called by the senator or governor."

Some of the materialists were more acceptable to the campaign organization than others. Those who continuously produced for the candidate were thought to have a right to a reward, and members of the staff would try to arrange one. However, as the field director of the Massachusetts campaign described it, "There is an element in the campaign that is interested in pursuing their own advancement politically. I'm not talking about those people who work every night, but the people who really haven't done anything but are interested in a pay-off in advance. They are people essentially concerned about security and long-term stability for themselves, finding a slot for themselves like those in a similar age bracket. Maybe they've been in and out of things: politicians who have run for several elective positions. There are some young fellows who fit into this category: people who have been in state government for six or eight years and are now looking for security."[10]

Although some of these people were part of the structure, others fell into another group that bore no continuous relationship to the political structure. Unlike those who had "been in and out of things," they were totally outside the political

---

[10]Interview with William Najam, Massachusetts field director, October 21, 1974.

world, and they had a conception of politics that was as idealized in a way as the conception held by the believers, though in a far more negative way. To them every favor ought to be associated with a reward, partly because they believed that was the way the game was played, and partly because they believed they would not have another opportunity to ask for or expect a reward. One man in Massachusetts, for example, was asked to let his home be used for a fund-raising party for the candidate. A businessman with few contacts among full-time political actors, he felt it would be the only opportunity he would have to express his desire to be named racing commissioner. As he put it, "When else would they come to me for anything?"

Because everyone in the campaign organization worked long, hard hours with few outside distractions, those who dealt with volunteers — who had to find time for their campaign activities over and above those of their daily lives — tended to become frustrated with their seeming lack of commitment. This would become a particularly sensitive point when the volunteer was also looking for something from the campaign, as the materialists did, and the problem was exacerbated when the outside materialists did not have the same sense of what was an appropriate reward for any given act as those who spent their lives in politics.

The Joiners

The joiners as a group were not very different from the believers, except that they did not express their motivation in terms of civic responsibility. As one of them quite directly put it, "I am working in the campaign as a chance to meet more people. It's not a meaningful thing." The joiners did, however, perform the same tasks as the believers.

Although the solidary rewards (which can be defined here as rewards that can be shared by anyone and are derived from the sociability that accompanies participation with others in the performance of routine tasks) were the motivating factors for the joiners to come into the campaign headquarters, the fact that they chose campaigns over other kinds of social activities means that they were not entirely untouched by the purposive incentives of the believer. As one woman who was a sixty-one-year-old schoolteacher put it, "Working in the public sector all the time you do meet people, but this is different: you meet people you agree with. You all see it almost the same."

Some of the joiners came back year after year to work in the campaigns. Others came because they were new to a community and were anxious to expand their field of acquaintances. Some came to meet other people and might not return once they found a compatible friend.

These, then, are the people who work in campaigns. The next two chapters will consider campaigns as organizations: first, how they establish and maintain themselves as structures; and second, how the structure functions to achieve the goal of electing the candidate. Having a sense of the backgrounds and expectations of the people will make the tasks and the difficulty of performing those tasks all the more understandable.

Chapter 4

The Campaign as an Organization

The purpose of a campaign is to elect a candidate, and its function is to stimulate the voters to that end. One might suppose, therefore, that most of the work of the campaign organization would.be directed toward the voters. Such, however, is not the case. Most of those who work in campaigns on a full-time basis perform tasks that are directed not at stimulating the voter, but at mobilizing resources — contributions of money and time from supporters of the candidate. In short, most of the campaign staff devotes most of its time to creating and maintaining the campaign organization, partly because some resources (especially money) are needed to reach the voters through the media and candidate travels, and partly because the local supporters of a candidate must themselves be organized so that (at a minimum) they do not make matters worse by calling public attention to their dissatisfactions or conflicts and (at the maximum) they become effective instruments for registering and bringing out the voters.

One can explain the behavior of campaigns, therefore, by explaining the tasks necessary to maintain the organization and the special conditions — here called the "organizational environment" — under which that maintenance must be achieved. It is because of the importance of these maintenance tasks that a visitor to a campaign organization is struck by how inward-looking the activities and thoughts of its members seem to be: the very opposite of what one expects if one assumed that, because winning is important, most activity and thinking is devoted to making rational calculations about how to identify and persuade the marginal voter to support the candidate. The very atmosphere and style of the campaign organization reinforces its inward-looking tendency and is the product of the tasks that must be performed and the environmental constraints on how the tasks are performed.

These two elements (the environment and the tasks) affect all campaigns and account for the similarity that exists in all campaign organizations, even to the extent of overcoming, to a degree, other characteristics such as the arrival of a new generation of political actors. These elements produce more organizational uniformity than one would predict knowing only the personality of the candidate, the party to which he or she belongs, and the office sought. And even though a campaign organization can be characterized as having a personalized or professionalized style, the style primarily reflects how an organization copes with one or the other of these two factors: a personalized campaign relieves the environmental uncertainty by stressing dependence on a single individual; a professionalized campaign is one that is focused on tasks. These relationships will be explored in this chapter.

The Environment

The most important environmental factors are these: *uncertainty,* which, owing to the difficulty of measuring the impact of campaign activities on the electorate, forces the organization to rely heavily on tradition (the things that worked in the past) and, paradoxically, to be at the same time open to any new ideas that are proposed, assuming there is the energy and persistence necessary to carry them out; a *limited organizational life*, which heightens the intensity of the experience for participants and discourages a hierarchical decision-making process, because there are few sanctions that can be imposed in so short-term an organization; and finally a *win/lose payoff*, which places an increasing weight on ends over means as the election draws near.[1]

Uncertainty is perhaps the most important of the environmental factors because it is the most pervasive. Even polling, which is designed to reduce uncertainty, rarely produces any agreement on what is required to win. The consequences of being bound by tradition on the one hand and open to new ideas on the other are that the organization is in a constant state of tension between those trying to hold to tradition (or at least to what they have already committed themselves to do) and those who are sometimes called "the savior of the week" — the people who come into the headquarters after having talked to the cab driver on the way over, and announce that they are in touch with "the People" (that is, the cab driver) and know what it will take "to turn this campaign around." If the idea is imaginative enough, if the organization is capable of doing it, and if there is someone with the persistence to do it, quite likely the idea will be implemented because no one can be certain that it will *not* "turn this whole campaign around." The tension between tradition and the "savior of the week" syndrome results in a proliferation of activities, many of which are unrelated to each other. These activities vie with each other for the campaign's limited resources.

The short-run nature of a campaign means that those who are drawn into the organization on a full-time basis are not bound to it out of habit, a sense of identity, or even a desire for money. Most people are hired to work in a campaign because they know someone already a part of the organization or someone with political influence. An organization that is made

---

[1]Xandra Kayden, "The Political Campaign as an Organization," *Public Policy*, vol. 21 (Spring 1973), no. 2.

up of people who are drawn into it because of their political alliances is in no position to assert much authority over those people, unless it is also willing to risk divisive consequences. Campaigns, therefore, rarely fire people. If someone is not doing a good job, the organization (assuming it can measure the quality of that individual's work) will prefer to supplement that person with someone else who will get the job done. Titles are easily given in campaigns, but they are not necessarily good measures of who is doing what, because an ineffectual individual with the title of "chairperson" may be supplemented by a "coordinator" who is actually doing the work.

The win/lose payoff of the campaign is the consequence of there being no second place in elections. A campaign that lays its strategy early and understands that its support will come from definable groups in the population will develop a rational approach to mobilizing those groups. As the election draws near, however, there is a tendency to believe that the candidate needs all the support he or she can get and to hope that the campaign can pick up support from a group heretofore neglected. If the candidate is in favor of, say, liberal abortion laws, and has built a campaign with the help of those who support that position, he or she will be in jeopardy of angering those supporters if the organization begins appealing to groups identified as being against that position. From the campaign perspective, the pro-abortion reform people may have no place to go — the other candidate could be worse on the issue. A new approach might lessen the hostility of the anti-abortion reformers and at least neutralize them, if not draw them into the list of active supporters. It is a trade-off whose benefits appear to outweigh its costs as the campaign gets closer and closer to the end.

Since campaign decisions tend to be made by whoever happens to be in the room at the time, *access* to the candidate or the campaign manager is a highly valued objective. One way to assure access is to be around a lot, and that is a major reason why the work of a campaign organization goes on late into the evening: no one wants to miss the opportunity to participate in a decision by leaving early. Power in the campaign organization is often a function of physical proximity; hence the location of the various parts of the campaign organization within the headquarters has an important effect on decisions. Campaign workers who share a room tend to form alliances with each other against those who work in other rooms. The farther one room is from another, the less likely people are to know about or understand the nature of the work done in those rooms.

There is a limit to this, however. If one part of the campaign is completely separated from another part because it is housed in another part of the city or another state (as advertising agencies often are), people will be curious about that distant part, but not particularly hostile to it. Such relationships were seen in Tennessee, as the campaign organization grew and offices were moved farther down the hall; in Indiana, where the car dealership in which the campaign was housed created a barrier in the form of the garage area that separated the financial offices from the political offices; and in Massachusetts, where the field organization felt isolated from the rest of the campaign organization, and most members of the campaign staff were unaware of the statehouse staff on the hill.

Campaign workers spend a lot of time in the organization — often sixteen hours a day, seven days a week. By spending so much time together, the campaign eliminates much of an individual's private life, causing him or her to rely more heavily on the organization for the kinds of supports and rewards normally found elsewhere. For most of the young organizers this was not a serious problem because they had relatively few external private commitments. Looking to each other for both professional and personal satisfactions may have added to their sense of being a group apart from others, a group engaged in a struggle. It was very clear, as one campaigner put it, that "when you spend that much time you become consumed in the organization. Something happens. You learn a lot about yourself: you are either going to exist in the organization or not. You have to be flexible. Being rigid would be emotionally very tough."

Clearly solidary rewards are important factors. For the campaign staff, these rewards were more intense than those found among the avocationalists, whose rewards could be called "collective" in that they could be enjoyed by anyone who came into the headquarters. The "specific" solidary reward for the staff is based on its group identity, which excludes others not part of the staff. In all three campaigns the separation between the vocationalists and the avocationalists was marked and can be explained by the difference between specific and collective solidary benefits.[2]

Jason Berman, Bayh's administrative assistant, noted the differences in receptivity to solidary rewards between the full-time members of the organization and the volunteers: "In order for campaigns to be successful they have to have an emotional link that is not necessarily present in making a successful business organization. They have to get out of people who work in the campaign more than they can give them. The only thing the campaign can give is that emotional link. . . . If you are in the campaign, the job responsibilities and tasks are such as to minimize the emotional and ideological commitment; whereas the farther away you are the more you have to rely on the emotional links, and the easiest way is around some personal identification with the candidate."

Berman was concerned, however, with the problem of separating the tasks created for the campaign staff, which causes the organization to lose some of the links necessary for coordination. He was looking for a mechanical solution. Perhaps the answer is to be found in the selective solidary rewards, the emotional linkage that grows up not around the candidate but among staff members and with the campaign as an organization.

The atmosphere in a campaign headquarters is informal. Everyone is on a first name basis, with the possible exception of the candidate. Because most campaign workers spend so much time at headquarters, the work flow is distributed throughout the day and evening at a rather uneven pace. People usually begin work fairly late in the morning (the Tennessee campaign was exceptional in starting around 8:30 A.M., perhaps a reflection of southern work habits and the differing time zones within the state) and gradually build up to a very busy period in the late afternoon. There is often a tapering-off

---

[2]James Q. Wilson, *Political Organizations* (New York: Basic Books, 1973), 33–34.

of work during the dinner hour, and it picks up again in the early evening, ending around 10 P.M. Crises, such as rush jobs to get a mailing out, can keep at least part of the staff working past midnight. There are always a few people to be found around the coffee machine, sharing the latest political gossip about polls or potential supporters and speculating about who is likely to have what job after the election. Walking into a campaign headquarters, one has the impression of a number of small groups of people actively or idly engaged in separate tasks. It is a busy environment, but one that also has time and space for relaxation.

The tasks in a campaign organization are often in conflict for the limited resources of money and candidate time. It is an inherent conflict given the short time frame of the campaign. Because this is an organizational study, it is focused on these conflicts. It is easy to describe the tensions that grow up within the organization because of the tasks and the mix of personalities those tasks require. As noted earlier, it is more difficult to describe the marked sense of solidarity that campaigns evoke in their workers. The importance of solidary rewards was, in fact, a significant conclusion in Eldersveld's book on Detroit politics.[3] It is for this reason that I would emphasize again, before beginning an analysis of the tasks, that to understand the nature of a campaign, one must understand that people participate in it because they find an intense emotional reward in their participation. For the avocationalists, the reward is dependent on their beliefs and their identification with the candidate or an ideology. For the vocationalists, the reward is found in the organization itself.

The Tasks

A campaign organization is created to demonstrate support for a candidate, generally through activities that are highly visible to the media. All three campaigns studied had about thirty full-time staff members in their central headquarters. Most of them were employed in either of the two major organization

---

[3]Samuel J. Eldersveld, *Political Parties* (Chicago: Rand McNally, 1964).

objectives: building a field organization or raising money. Subsidiary tasks included those that handled logistics of either the candidate or the campaign (scheduling, press, clerical support), and those that were geared toward special constituencies, such as the party, labor unions, blacks, youth, farmers, and so on — identifiable groups in the population that were likely to endorse one candidate over another. Another category of campaign activity was research and speech writing, closely allied to the press department, with access to the key decision makers and the candidate. That group will be discussed in the next chapter. The tasks described in this chapter are those of maintaining the organization: the voluntary field organization, fund raising, lining up special groups of supporters, and clerical work.

Most of the work of a campaign is routine, labor intensive, and similar from one campaign to the next or from one local headquarters to the next. There are some important decisions to be made, and many more minor decisions, which, because of the routine nature of most of the activity, may have the impact of major decisions. How the organization differentiates between major and minor decisions depends to a large extent on its structure: a personalized campaign organization pushes most decisions to the top, to be made by the head of the organization or the candidate (as in Tennessee); a professionalized campaign breaks down the tasks into clearly divisible areas of responsibility, and decisions rise to the top only when there is conflict between the various parts of the organization (as in Indiana). All campaigns have some division of responsibility according to tasks, and because the structure is never so clearly defined in terms of a chain of command, even professionalized campaigns will be confused by decisions being made at all levels without regard to the formal structure.

Some of the tasks are compatible with each other and some are competitive. But wherever there is division according to task (even when the tasks are inherently compatible), there is conflict. Presumably this is true of all organizations, but it is particularly noticeable in campaigns because the temporary nature of the activity makes it unlikely that the priorities or the organization as a whole will be reflected in work patterns. One reason it is unlikely is that priorities for the organization change very quickly from week to week in a campaign, depending on when the major campaign events are scheduled or external pressures, such as busing in Boston, or the drawing near of the election. Another reason is that the uncertain environment in which a campaign operates makes it almost impossible to demonstrate the value of one task over another, and what gets done may depend on who in the organization asked for help when.

When there is inherent competition between tasks, the job of settling priorities becomes even more difficult. This is particularly true in the two major functions of fund raising and building a field organization. As noted by Jason Berman, "They are both identified as self-important contained entities, and they fight over time and resources."

Another area likely to evoke organizational conflict relates to the mix of personalities and tasks. It became quite evident during this study that campaign tasks can be divided into two categories: those that require exact measures and attention to detail; and those that are unmeasurable and show little visible return. The people who perform the first category of tasks tended to be concerned with efficiency and to find satisfaction in their jobs when they could demonstrate their organized methods. The people who were responsible for the second category of tasks tended to have a high tolerance for ambiguity. There is a potential for organizational conflict between these approaches to the job, as in Indiana, and there is potential for unhappiness on the job when the right personality is not matched with the right task.

The Field Organization

When we speak of campaigning, we generally think of a candidate going out to meet the voters, attend rallies of his or her supporters, and so on. The campaign itself becomes part of the message: a message in this case that suggests enthusiastic support for the candidate, as well as indicating what he or she stands for by making public which leaders in a community support the candidacy. The field organization makes possible the events at which the candidate appears in towns across the state and identifies the candidate's supporters, which is particularly important if those supporters are to be mobilized to cast their ballots on election day.

This study is about the campaign organization found in the central headquarters, not the field organization. Nonetheless it is important to say a few words about the task of the field organization, a traditional one in American politics. The tradition was based originally on the party system, especially on the ward politics typical of our urban areas, where local political figures played significant roles in mediating between the people and the institutions.

Theoretically, the field organization works along with the party, supplementing the continuous party organization with temporary help. In recent years, the tendency has been for the permanent and temporary organizations to operate independently of each other, though there are some tasks that require party involvement because of state election laws — particularly voter registration. As one campaign worker described the relationships, "The function of the party is to complain about the organization. You cannot trust the party apparatus to get something done. In some areas you can, but you have to be careful and know who's involved."

Probably the single greatest reason for this separation of organizations has been the growth of primary elections, which require each candidate to mount his or her own organization within the party. The winning candidate, then, is faced with having to reunite the party by bringing in to the campaign the supporters of all the primary opponents, as well as the party officials who were neutral during the primary race. It is not difficult to understand the strain this puts on the original organization, particularly when the division of supporters during the primary between candidates reflected a factional split in the party organization at the local level to begin with. This was seen clearly in the Tennessee campaign, when the state field organization was pressured to choose between rival factions at the county level.

Another reason for the split between the party and the campaign organization is the difference in age between the campaign professionals and the party leadership, a difference that may be on the average as much as thirty years. Nowhere is that split felt more acutely than in the field organization, when young campaign workers are put in the position of telling older party leaders what their jobs will be and when they will have access to the candidate.

There are three major organizational problems for the field: (1) the creation of a temporary volunteer organization, which vies with other activities in the daily life of the volunteer worker; (2) testing the operation to be sure it is functional on election day, usually by assigning measurable tasks that give visibility to the organization as well as the candidate; and (3) defining those tasks in such a way as to have the largest possible effect upon the voters in the state.

Creation of a Temporary Voluntary Organization

At the state headquarters level, the name of the political game is getting people *into* the organization. At the county level and below, however, there are many eager to keep some people *out*. The resources that will be distributed to the victor are, after all, limited and, at the local level particularly, they tend to be concrete and visible. This conflict between the desire at the top for the organization to expand and the desire in the middle to keep it small and elite is probably the greatest source of difficulty between the political staff of the candidate and the materialist volunteers in the field. As Jim Miller, the field representative for a Tennessee congressman, put it: "Victory is a great thing. And it's real hard. It takes elasticity in a person to get other people in. You have to give and take a great deal to get other people in." Giving and taking for the materialists at the local level is not necessarily hard, especially if they control the concrete rewards such as jobs, low-number license plates, or measurable prestige. It is more difficult, however, if those rewards are controlled at the state level, as they often are. When rewards are distributed to local supporters and the local organization is not involved in that distribution, it lowers the prestige and the political strength of the local leadership.

From the campaign perspective, working with the field was

essentially a fence-mending occupation. All three campaigns faced factional rivalries at the local level, but Tennessee was the most representative of the problem because the Republican party was just old enough, it appeared, to have developed factions. As one observer noted: "The real problem is the difference in understanding who these people [the rival factions] are and how they perceive themselves and the importance of the political situation. If they've been included for six or eight years and suddenly find themselves empty-handed, they are frustrated and you don't even know who they are."

Campaigns mend fences by allocating rewards. The organization, however, is always beset by uncertainty about to whom those rewards ought to be allocated, because a long-standing personal relationship with the local people is usually lacking. There is a natural tendency to appoint the people one knows to positions of responsibility. When the field staff in the headquarters does not even know the names of those at the local level who traditionally held those responsibilities, they can do more harm than good. Field organizations are, of course, rarely so ill informed as to not know the names of the traditional participants. But there can be other reasons for appointing one person over another that have the same effect: if one person was an early supporter and the other did not want to join the campaign until late; if one person had personal supporters at the state level who advocated his or her interests over a rival's; or if the campaign sought someone because he or she had other valuable attributes, such as a constituency built around an issue, or an image that seemed more appropriate to the candidate than the traditional leadership image would have been.

Factionalism is not the only problem that campaign organizations face when it comes to "getting people in" at the local level. Even if there are no warring parties, there are conflicts for the individuals involved between their desire to participate, on the one hand, and the everyday demands on their time and energy, on the other. A member of the Indiana organization described it this way: "When you have paid people with responsibility to which they are exclusively committed — a fundamental job — you have a need, or a concept, of a highly structured program to be effected. But you are relying on people out there to be able to carry out your program without knowing very much about their time, or much other than their past affiliations. You don't know the degree of their commitment. They are not like a hired staff where you have the controls of hiring and firing. The regional people feel highly responsible and totally motivated, and you get varying degrees of that on the county level. Those who carry through — that depends on personal commitment and time, and effectiveness in terms of communication."[4]

Although a number of people in the campaigns pointed to the distinction between paid and unpaid workers (most suggesting that though motivated volunteers were better than paid staff, there were controls that could be exercised over paid workers), I tend to think that the economic distinction is irrelevant. It is not the money, it is the personal commitment and time that matter most. As one paid staff member in Massachusetts noted, "There is a kind of job security in campaigns because there is no security: you know you are going to be out of a job come November, so what difference does it make?"

The difference between doing something full-time and doing something part-time is probably the most important distinction. Full-time people will be committed — especially those who work "sixteen hours a day, seven days a week" — because the social pressures within the organization will be intense, and probably far more effective than economic rewards, particularly when those rewards are generally sparse to begin with. It is not unusual for a staff member to be paid somewhere between $50 and $100 a week. Many will get less (a few will get more). The temporary nature of the organization also makes the economic reward less significant.

It may also be that commitment is partly a function of the degree of dislocation the campaign causes in people's lives. Those people, for example, who came to Indiana from Bayh's Senate staff in Washington, who lived together in the same apartment complex and had no calls upon their time from family and friends or any sense of civic responsibility, were com-

---

[4]Interview with George Nelson, Indiana staff member, October 4, 1974.

mitted to the campaign as a way of life. Those people who worked at home in their own counties, adding campaign responsibilities to the long list of other activities that drew them to the attention of the regional coordinators in the first place, would have the most difficult time setting aside the hours in the day and night it takes to perform campaign chores. And, of course, the more local the campaign, the more particular the tasks, and the more difficult they are to accomplish. It is one thing to sit in a state headquarters and decide whether or not to try to raise money by passing around paper buckets with the candidate's name pasted on the side. It is quite another to carry the bucket to your next-door neighbor and ask for a donation.

The statewide organization has to develop incentives to motivate the field organization. One is the distribution of goods and services that appeals to the materialists; another is the satisfaction of the tasks themselves. For the organization, however, there is always tension between the desire to allow enough autonomy to the field organization to enable people to express their creativity and display their political talents, on the one hand, and the desire of the organization to control from the center what happens on the periphery, on the other. As the lieutenant governor of Massachusetts, Donald Dwight, put it: "Centralization versus decentralization tensions are endemic to any large organization. Things take pendulum swings: you let things decentralize until they go too far. A case could be made for strong central control, but it's demoralizing for the person in the field. When you have no control, however, people believe that what they are doing is *the* most important thing — to them, the whole election will turn on whether or not the candidate gets into their whistle stop."[5]

The problem was manifest in Massachusetts because of the need felt early in the campaign to centralize and exercise discipline, and because of the bureaucratic style of the head of the field organization. Members of the field staff, as well as people in the field, had little say in the decision process. One staff person quoted a field worker as saying, "Whenever the phone rings, it's a call to stand out [holding signs] or sit down

---

[5] Interview on November 7, 1974.

[for office chores]. No one asks what I think." The need to be responsive to local issues and local pressures is balanced against the need to create a statewide organization. Each side may think the other too parochial and bound too much by its environment. The people who lived on Cape Cod, for instance, did not understand why the whole campaign had to come to a stop during the busing crisis in Boston.

The frustration was illustrated by the campaign manager in Tennessee, who said of one of the regional coordinators, "That guy takes too much on himself. He's trying to act like a bigger boy than he is." And two days later said of the same person: "If we had more guys like him we would be in fine shape."

One reason the tension between centralization and decentralization is constant is that a local political organization may be running candidates of its own. Furthermore, issues of concern in one part of a state may not be relevant in another. Even if the local organization was created by the campaign and is not part of an on-going party structure, once people are brought together to form an organization, they tend to think of their task as one among many they will perform in the future, and they go on as individuals with political interests even if they do not stay together as an organization.

Bayh's administrative assistant described the problem for the campaign organization this way: "There is a communications problem between the people who are professionally a part of the campaign and the people who are 'involved' in the campaign — the various groups that support the candidate. How do you tell a county chairman that this is what is best — or a labor union president?" The creation of a field organization depends on being able to "tell a county chairman" what is best, the autonomy of the various parts notwithstanding. But the strain has its effect on the people within the campaign, as a field worker noted: "You become politically an animal. You look at people in terms of what they can do for you today. How can you get votes out of them? It's something we play to accomplish certain goals. The ends of those means are good enough, hopefully. If you win, it's fine, but if you lose, it is tough."

All three campaigns felt the tension that comes from the

strains of centralization versus decentralization. Whether the field organizers worked along with the party, as in Indiana, or tried to mend party factionalism, as in Tennessee, or sought to heal a split between the campaign and the party, as in Massachusetts, the strains were there; and it was, as the head of the Massachusetts field organization, Bill Najum, described it, "a people-to-people job. . . . The greatest challenge has been knowing how to treat people a certain way in order to get the job done."[6] Sometimes the field organization thrived on the challenge, as one staff member noted: "You get a great deal of pleasure motivating 128 people to get up at 6:00 A.M. to stand out and hold signs from 7:00 to 9:00 in the morning." And sometimes it made them feel "politically like an animal."

Testing the Field Organization

Everything the traditional field organization does is geared to election day. In order to ensure the smoothest possible functioning in the field on that day, tasks are assigned for it to perform during the course of the campaign to test its organizational strength and to build up enthusiasm for the big day.

Although there is often variation from year to year in the kinds of tasks undertaken by the field, most are done because they were done before. The uncertainty as to what actually makes a difference in an election campaign renders tradition particularly appealing, and traditions may be, therefore, the single most important determinant of what a field organization actually does. The tasks assigned the field to test its organizational strength have to meet several requirements: they must be labor intensive; they must be easily replicable; they must require few props; and they should appear to be an organized, enthusiastic commitment by some of the state's voters. Voter registration is the prime example of a necessary task that meets these criteria. Other tasks are less necessary but are performed to "give the field a shot in the arm," as the political consultant in Tennessee described it, "so they can be sure they are not alone."[7]

---

[6] Interview with William Najam, Massachusetts field director, October 21, 1974.
[7] Interview with Clifford White, Tennessee campaign consultant, September 30, 1974.

Most campaigns establish local headquarters for their field operations, often in vacant stores or other buildings on main thoroughfares in a community. The offices are decorated with large signs and posters of the candidate in the windows. If volunteers are available, the storefronts will be kept open for passersby to come in to ask questions and gather literature about the campaign, and as a place for volunteers to meet, get out mailings, and canvass by telephone. If a campaign is unable to provide the volunteer force to keep these headquarters open, campaign workers still believe they benefit from the visibility the posters and signs provide.

Having the space and the desire to "bring people in," the campaign field organization is always faced with the problem of giving them something to do that is beneficial to the campaign and relatively rewarding to the volunteer. The labor-intensive nature of campaign tasks is especially designed for that purpose. The tasks that were used in the three campaigns included voter registration (done in conjunction with the party); gathering signatures for the candidate to run in the primary; telephoning known and unknown supporters (telephone lists coming either from voter registration rolls, previous campaign lists, or the telephone book); distributing literature, bumper stickers, yard signs (large cardboard posters that can be set on a lawn, in a window, or around a street pole), or car tops (cardboards signs not unlike bumper stickers that are stapled to form a triangle and are strapped to the top of cars — more expensive but also more visible than bumper stickers), campaign buttons, and general information about voting.

Additional tasks that appeared to be particularly in vogue were special programs designed to individualize the campaign by having volunteers send postcards or notes to their friends saying they were supporting the candidate. The interesting thing about this effort was that it was relatively inexpensive for the campaign (which did supply the writing materials) and probably very effective, given what we know about how voters make up their minds. Although people normally vote according to their party identification — which can be predicted by demographic information — they are most likely to be swayed by informal opinion leaders within their social or professional circle. The Indiana campaign, which was the most task oriented of the three studied, also had a fairly extensive voter identification program that relied on volunteers' telephoning potential voters, identifying likely supporters, and sending them information on issues in which they were interested.

What all these tasks had in common was that they could be performed with a minimum amount of training (explicit instructions were always included in the special programs, such as voter identification or note day), they could be done almost any time during the course of the campaign, and they did not require a long-term commitment from a volunteer — one could telephone for one evening or every evening, depending on how much time the volunteer wanted to give the campaign. The tasks could also be performed by any number of volunteers, from one up to as many as the headquarters had room for or the voting population allowed. They could be performed by the high-level volunteers who were part of the formal structure of the campaign field organization, or they could be performed by the incidental visitors to the campaign headquarters who might or might not have an expectation of returning. One of the phenomena of recent political history has been the development in presidential primary campaign organizations of people who act as mobilizing cadres, going from one primary state to another setting up field organizations. This is possible because the tasks are so routine and replicable it does not matter who the people are who perform them.

Volunteers prove their worth to the campaign organization by performing more, rather than by doing things better. As the deputy head of the Massachusetts field operation put it: "Fortunately, we started out early in the campaign with a concrete measure of people's performances. Those who excelled on the signatures have been the good guys in the sense of producing all the way through. Those that didn't have been the bad guys."[8] Whether the "good guy" went out and got 1,000 signatures by himself or organized 100 volunteers to do so is irrelevant to the campaign organization. Presumably, it would make a difference whether or not the signatures were of bona

[8]Interview with James Velis, Massachusetts assistant field director, October 30, 1974.

fide voters, but one finds that out so long after the event it is organizationally insignificant.

Defining the Tasks to Have an Effect upon the Voters

A "good campaign" in the eyes of its field workers is one that runs well mechanically: it distributes so much literature in so many neighborhoods, makes so many telephone calls, and so on. One can run a good campaign in that sense and still lose the election. But winning is not the only reward for the volunteers in the field organization. It is entirely possible that for many it is a secondary objective. How one does one's job in the political arena may be far more important to the individual because it will have an impact on what he or she is asked to do next time, and what rewards he or she is offered should the candidate win.

There is great uncertainty whether a "good campaign" wins votes. As one field staff member in Massachusetts described it, "You can get 5,000 bumper stickers out in one day, but does that affect the vote? So then you have to measure your success in bumper stickers. The finance department can measure in dollars, but which one leads to a vote? Are stand-outs the best use of people's time? You press people to work as hard as they can to show as much as you can that there are people out there who support the governor."

One way of handling the uncertainty, and thereby lessening the sense of isolation that uncertainty creates in people who work in the field, was described by the head of the Indiana field organization. He spoke of having a "sense of unease" that was relieved only by his belief "that the way to do the job was to build rapport, establish credibility and trust that his own sense of integrity would be matched by others."[9] The unease and sense of isolation are due to the intense focus on these measurable tasks, which made campaign workers feel isolated from others in the campaign who were not working on the same task. Many campaign workers were indeed isolated, speaking only to their own supporters. But if the tasks did not

---

[9]Interview with David Bochnowski, Indiana field director, October 3, 1974.

change a vote (some were designed to do so more than others), they did provide feedback to the organization on the degree of support the candidate had anyway. If crowds came to rallies, if a large proportion of those canvassed said they would vote for the candidate, if many bumper stickers were seen on cars — all these signs were assurances that the campaign was going in the right direction. And if they did not measure up to past experience, the field organization was urged to work harder. The larger question of what it was that brought people out or made them feel enough of a sense of identity with the candidate to put his bumper sticker on their cars was not asked by the campaign leaders, though it may well have been asked by the field workers or by the voters.

Very rarely does a field organization face the opposition. That fact points up another aspect of the relationship of the field organization to the vote: the field activity is focused on its own supporters, and more energy and more of the campaign's resources (especially the candidate's time) will be spent in those areas of the state where the candidate's or the party's strength has traditionally been the strongest. Alexander, for example, spent about half his time in east Tennessee, which had under a third of the state's population but more than half of the Republican voters in the state. The function of the field becomes, then, not so much to convince the opponent's supporters but to encourage one's own. Occasionally, field activities will be mounted for tactical effect, as the campaign chairman in Tennessee noted about an area of the state that traditionally voted Democratic: "Any activity there would drive Ray Blanton out of his skull."[10]

Even though the field organization focuses its activity on its supporters, and even though it does sometimes play a role in the gamesmanship of politics by performing tactical maneuvers, a number of volunteers also want to "get" the opposition candidate. As one of the Tennessee field staff noted, "There is a little unrest among the troops. It is hard for the local county people to get a grasp of the statewide effort. County folks want to do something and they don't know where to go."[11] Some-

---

[10]Interview with Hal Carter, Tennessee campaign chairman, September 30, 1974.
[11]Interview with John Crowe, Tennessee field worker, September 28, 1974.

times people would come into the state headquarters with negative information about the opposition; sometimes they would use the information themselves. Part of the desire to "get" the enemy was a result of the spirit of warfare a campaign evokes in people's minds, particularly in the minds of those who are more distant from the center of the operation. And part of the desire was based on the belief of those people on the periphery that this was what politics is all about: showing the weak underbelly of the enemy.

A number of people on the field staff in each campaign spoke of the need to contain that desire to "turn this campaign around and really show him up for what he is." Not only did the staff want to protect their candidate and campaign from charges ranging from libel to dirty politics, but also they wanted to present a different image of the campaign, an image that was positive, an image of an effective professional organization. It is quite likely, furthermore, that any idea that came from outside the central staff would be suspect just because it threatened to divert energy away from the tasks and therefore had some implications for the campaign's sense of its own integrity.

One way the campaign copes with this pressure to go after the opposition is to "take the information under advisement"; another is to focus everyone's energy so heavily on the tasks that they derive satisfaction from their own strength and visibility. The Tennessee organization, which was the least task-oriented of the three campaigns, came up with the idea of a statewide bumper sticker and statewide pole sign days after just such a meeting with local people. A third way the campaign copes with negative information, of course, is to use it, or, preferably, to get someone in the media to use it — someone who would not be accused of playing dirty politics.

Fund Raising

Fund raising is one of the few campaign tasks that is not beset by uncertainty: either the money is coming in or it is not. The consequence of lessening the uncertainty is that it enables fund raisers to be more creative in their work, or at least to be responsive to new methods developed by others.

If it is true that there are cycles or fads in politics, 1974 was the year of campaign financial disclosures. A few years previously it had been polling, and before that the use of the media — both of which have become part of the fabric of politics by now. New campaign funding laws and the greater awareness of political morality brought about by the Watergate scandal combined in 1974 to make campaigners very conscious of how they raised money, from whom they accepted it, and how they made public their lists of contributors.

As is true of most political activity, there is a certain mystique to fund raising, and those who are not involved in financing campaigns have an inordinate amount of respect and awe for those who are. The mysteriousness of political activity is probably due to the distance most people have from the day-to-day functioning of the political process, and the sense that somehow political actors create realities out of wisps and snaps of things. There are few things in campaigns as concrete as money; those with a reputation for being able to get money carry great weight.

All three campaigns sought to raise and spend about a million dollars. They succeeded in raising about the same amount in the campaign period, somewhere between $800,000 and $900,000. Indiana was the most successful in keeping within a budget, largely because the Bayh organization was determined not to go into debt, as it had six years before. The Massachusetts campaign was least successful in spending within the set limit, because financial controls were not given much priority, those who raised money did not make decisions on how to spend it, and there had always been enough in the past. The Alexander campaign in Tennessee was closer to Indiana in controls; although the campaign ended with a debt of $52,000, the staff ultimately raised more than enough to enable them to close their books in the black.

Campaigns raise money by a combination of four methods:

1. *Person-to-person contact,* preferably someone of influence calling upon his or her associates. As Ted Welch, the co-chairman of the Tennessee finance department, put it, "Influence, like water, flows down. We tried to determine who our bell cows were — the people who will

give at a high level — because they set the standard for everyone else."

2. *Direct mail solicitation,* a fairly recent application of computer technology that enables a campaign to develop lists of people interested in specific issues and to solicit their support for the candidate, based on a common interest.

3. *Fund-raising affairs,* which can be anything from small fund-raising dinners or cocktail parties to large-scale entertainment productions, such as the Indiana jazz concert.

4. *Special relationships,* recognition of large givers by including them in groups like governor's clubs, which implies they have special access to the candidate. In Indiana large givers to the Bayh campaign were sent plaques commemorating their contribution; in Massachusetts there was an effort to expand the governor's club, which had numbered a little over a hundred prior to the 1974 campaign; and in Tennessee the Alexander campaign made a political issue of the governor's club of the opposition and preferred less formal recognition of their heavy givers.

The person-to-person and the special relationship methods are characteristic of politics of the "old school." Each is mysterious in its own way, especially the former, because the fund raiser's ability to produce is dependent as much on his or her approach as it is on the candidate's intrinsic worth. Victor Zuchero, Sargent's permanent fund raiser, was a representative of the traditional approach; part of the difficulty the rest of the campaign staff had with Zuchero was bound up with the mystery he maintained about who gave what.

The fund-raising affairs require considerable organizational ability, and even then, external variables can intervene to make the affair a failure, especially if it is a large-scale effort designed to sell several thousand tickets. The black fund-raising concert in Indiana, for example, was complicated not only by poor communication within the organization, but by the peculiar circumstance of having several well-known entertainers come to town at about the same time the concert was planned to take place — a situation that was quite unusual in Indianapolis. The success or failure of such large-scale efforts is also complicated by the commitment the campaign must make to them in "up front" money — financial resources that will enable the planners to purchase the material and advertising the affair requires. If, for example, a concert is expected to net the campaign $50,000 after expenses, and it only breaks even, those items in the budget that were to be funded by the concert's profits are in serious jeopardy. All organizations suffer something of a cash flow problem, but it is a severe problem for a campaign. As someone said of the Massachusetts county fair fund raiser, "It was a success in that it produced more than it cost. It was an absolute failure in that it produced less than was projected."

Less time-consuming for the campaign, and often more rewarding in terms of a balance of costs and benefits, are the smaller fund-raising affairs. Usually they are given in someone's home and the guest list is carefully selected. There is a status appeal in these smaller fund raisers, as there is to those that fit under the "special recognition" category. People give not just because they want to see a particular candidate elected but because they want to be thought of as givers, as people of influence themselves. Although such events normally require the presence of the candidate, at least for some portion of the day or evening, other supports are usually provided by those outside the campaign headquarters staff. In 1974 events of this sort were still profitable financially, but potentially costly politically. An important objective of much of the fund raising in 1974 was to expand the base of contributors — to collect smaller amounts from many more people, and public reports of the traditional small fund-raising dinners and cocktail parties could be detrimental to the image of a "people's candidate."

A notable exception in the fund-raising affairs category were the "People for Alexander Parties," which were designed specifically to elicit the small contribution from a broad spectrum of people who normally did not contribute to political campaigns. Developed by David White for the Tennessee gubernatorial race, the parties sought to get money in a less formal, though still social context. It is interesting to note that they appeared to be more successful in the rural sections of the state than in the urban areas. According to one of those involved in the planning of these parties, "In the large cities people are hesitant to give parties and charge people for coming, but in some of the smaller counties they are eating it up."[12] Perhaps because the "charge" was minimal, urban dwellers felt it was too unsophisticated for them.

Still, the "People for Alexander Parties" were a variation on a theme, and the theme was more typical of the older fund-raising style. The newer trends were in the direction of the direct mail approach. Because fund raising is not subject to the same uncertainty that besets so much of what a campaign does, people can experiment with new technologies and new approaches. The Indiana campaign had perhaps the most sophisticated application of technology and innovation in fund raising, partly because the staff had the experience of several campaigns behind them as an organization, but also because they expected Senator Bayh to be in Washington for most of the campaign period with the impeachment trial. With little expectation of being able to use the candidate for fund raising, they built their finance campaign around the use of lists, carefully drawn to give the campaign the best possible sense of how much to expect from whom.

The major talisman for fund raising is "the List." As someone in Indiana put it, after noting that their lives seemed to be focused entirely on the accumulation of lists: "We've got so many lists we could set them to music, open in Hartford, and sell them to Ribicoff. . . ." Selling lists is, in fact, another way campaigns raise money, though usually after the campaign is over.

There is rarely a time when an incumbent or an expectant candidate is not trying to raise money for the pending campaign, so the fund-raising season is not quite so limited in time as the general campaign. All three organizations went into their campaigning with a "kitty" from which they could draw to begin hiring a staff and raise more money. The fact that they

---

[12]Interview with Roger Kelsey, Tennessee finance worker, October 1, 1974.

had money to begin with — and money that was raised in easier economic and political times — probably affected the erroneous sense that money would not be too difficult to raise as long as one went about it with as much sophistication as possible.

How campaigns spend the money they raise is an important organizational question. According to Roland Cole in *Campaign Spending in Senate Elections*, there are four categories of activities: "paid-media activities, free-media activities, worker-contact activities, and candidate-contact activities. No campaign in 1972 [the period of the Cole study] concentrated on one of these categories to the exclusion of the others, but each had its own combination of the four."[13] Although it is not a simple matter to gather reliable information from available campaign-spending reports (testified to by the Cole study), of the three campaigns in the present study, the major categories appeared to come under two headings: media expenses (primarily paid-media); and organizational expenses (staff, rent, and so on), mostly for the staff at the state headquarters.

Other factors about raising and spending money for the organization are the timing — when most money comes and how the campaign handles its cash flow — and the tendency for there to be greater demands on money at the end, when the election is near and a number of last-minute ideas are competing with each other for available resources. After the original resources are used up, there is usually some money coming in, but the biggest period of return in fund raising is the last two weeks before the election, when many events take place and when people are more excited about the end of the race. The relatively dry period between the beginning and end is usually handled by delaying payment on bills or by lowering expectations of how much to spend on various items in the budget. The Bayh campaign, for example, went off the air three or four times during the course of the campaign (in fact, it was not on the air during the period of the study in the first half of October) because it did not have the income it expected. And

---

[13]Roland Cole, "Campaign Spending in Senate Elections" (Ph.D. dissertation, Kennedy School of Government, Harvard University, 1975), 209.

larger budget items (none is larger than that for media) are easier to chip away at than smaller items that might have to be cut out altogether. Bill Wise, Bayh's press secretary, attended as many finance meetings as he could, to protect the media budget from just that kind of chipping. As he described it, he wanted to be able to defend his budget on the one hand, and on the other, he did not want those in the meeting to decide to cut the media and then develop a sense of group solidarity around their decision because he was not there in the first place.

It is interesting and organizationally significant to note that while a campaign may cut the media budget because it is large and more abstract (it is easier to decide to spend $10,000 less on an item budgeted at $250,000 than on one budgeted at $12,000), the campaign does not take a similar view toward the other large item in the budget: the organizational expenses — salary and rent. Salaries are anything but abstract. Firing people who were hired because they were friends of someone with influence, or have influence in their own right, can have political ramifications for the tone of the campaign as it is perceived by those people one is trying to attract. For those inside the organization, there may be a limit to the amount of uncertainty with which one can cope: the intensity of the organizational experience and the consequent feeling of belonging to a team probably lessen the difficulty of coping with the external uncertainty. Destroying that sense of belonging may be organizationally more debilitating than any outside influences, including polls and other indications that the candidate is not likely to win the election. A campaign in dire straits may cut salaries in half, or even stop paying people for varying lengths of time, but it will go to great lengths to avoid firing anyone.

The desire to minimize internal uncertainty was one of the reasons the operations manager in Indiana hired temporary clerical help: "Things cannot work by hiring friends of politicians, only by hiring people who are outside the group and who will remain outside. Volunteers are here because they want to be part of something — people who are hungry for attention. The operation can be depersonalized and you can accomplish more with this type of person [paid workers]. They have no hangups. They come to work. If you want something done right you can't have volunteers do it. If you have to let someone go, they get the whole tribe upset over one typist."[14] Whether or not the organization can in fact be "depersonalized" by hiring outsiders is questionable. For one thing, they may not remain outsiders, and for another, I suspect it is that sense of belonging and personal commitment that holds the organization together in the first place. Atkinson was generally successful in keeping his clerical staff outside the mainstream of the campaign, partly because they worked in separate offices and partly because they were a group of women who came from a temporary agency in which they were part owners and had their own sense of organizational loyalty. It was also true that they were black and most of the campaign staff was white.

The relative standing of department heads in the campaign organization could also be a factor in deciding which items in the budget to cut. In Massachusetts, for example, a tense conversation took place late in the campaign between Al Kramer, the chief policy advisor, and Steve Crosby, the campaign manager, over how they would raise the money for a half-hour television program Kramer wanted produced. When asked how they were going to get the money for it, Kramer responded by suggesting they "cut the campaign staff." Crosby replied that cutting the staff would only net them $14,000. Kramer said he was "only kidding," and went on to ask about other expenses that might be trimmed. Wise in Indiana would never have suggested cutting the campaign staff, even in jest, because of his more tenuous position among the staff in the organization.

Another strain on the budget was the proliferation of bright ideas, especially toward the end of the campaign. One reason for the proliferation of ideas at the end of the campaign is that communications are better; even more important, people have been engaged enough by the process to have given some thought to what ought to happen, especially in the context of

---

[14]Interview with Robert Atkinson, Indiana operations manager, October 2, 1974.

what has or has not happened. There is also a far greater sense of urgency in the last two weeks than there is when the campaign has two months yet to go. Another factor may be the somewhat paradoxical one that there appears to be more money available in the last two weeks than at other times. If it is true that most fund raising pays off then, campaign workers are more aware of the rise in income, and less aware of debts that were accrued earlier in the campaign — debts that were to be paid with this last-minute income.

As is true of a number of activities a campaign undertakes, the medium is the message in campaign finance. How the organization seeks to raise money says a lot about how that candidate expects to conduct himself or herself in office. This is particularly true in the post-Watergate and post-McGovern era. In Tennessee, the campaign organization refused to take contributions from those who would not consent to public disclosure — a difficult situation for those who might have something to gain from supporting the incoming governor no matter which candidate won (true of contractors in general, and apparently true of real estate interests in the state in the period of the study). In Massachusetts, also a gubernatorial race, the campaign fund raisers said they would not accept contributions from labor, lobbyists, or public employees. Clearly a governor is far more significant in the distribution of goods and services than a member of the United States Senate, hence the differences in values as to who is or is not an acceptable contributor. But most of the sensitivity to the issue is due to the implications of public disclosure and the heightened public awareness of campaign finance.

In Massachusetts, for example, where the campaign finance law is one of the more stringent in the nation, not only the governor but also the leading candidate for secretary of state, who had drafted the legislation when he was a state representative, were caught by technical violations of the law as then interpreted. The Indiana campaign, which was bound by federal campaign finance law, spent considerable energy during the course of the campaign compiling the records required by law. The staff filed a 1,300-page report on their finances by the end of August, the period prior to the main focus of energy of the general campaign.

All this is not to suggest that campaign finance regulation is inappropriate, but rather that it was a factor in the organizational distribution of energy and resources in the 1974 campaigns because of its newness, and because temporary organizations probably have greater difficulty coping with detailed reports than permanent organizations. The Tennessee campaign employed a full-time accountant just to handle the reports. Because the campaign organizations were so conscious of what their lists of contributors would look like to the public, they were probably far more sensitive in 1974 than they had ever been before — and perhaps will ever be again — to how they asked for money and from whom they accepted it.

Special Groups

An important function of a campaign is to demonstrate how widespread support is for its candidate. The field organization is one clear demonstration (and the substructure of the finance organization throughout the state is often another, perhaps less overt demonstration). The organization of special groups is a third method. Such groups are often pre-existing, and either they will endorse the candidate or some of their members will. A primary assumption about organizing them is that the candidate has some tie to the group by origin, experience, or promise for the future.

Groups are organized according to *ethnic origin* (blacks, Spanish-speaking, Italians); *professional association* (doctors, lawyers, farmers, labor unions); *age and sex* (youth, senior citizens, women); *issue concern* (gun control, right-to-life, conservationists); and *political identification* (independents, liberals, mayors, Democrats for Sargent/Alexander, Republicans for Bayh). All three campaigns organized groups. They appear to be particularly common in Democratic campaigns because of the constituency nature of that party; the Bayh campaign not only organized groups but had their representatives on the staff as a demonstration of commitment to the idea of that group as a special constituency.

The most important groups are those already organized that can assist the campaign by reaching out to their membership through their own structures. Labor unions are the best representative of these groups, and although they may not be able to endorse the candidate publicly, they can do so privately, which is to say they can make recommendations to their own membership on how to vote. The relationship of organized labor to the Democratic party is well known and goes back many years.[15] The consequences for a statewide campaign — assuming one can generalize from the Bayh experience — are that labor can provide financial support (both from the national and the local union organizations); it can endorse candidates and educate union membership to the importance of voting for a candidate; it can encourage more active participation by organizing volunteers to work with the field organization or with their own union membership; and it can lend full-time workers to a campaign. Significantly, a United Auto Workers bylaw requires union officeholders to participate in politics. The regulation does not require more than voting, but the high percentage of union leadership that does participate (particularly within the party structure) is indicative of the influence the unions exert in that direction.

Groups that center around demographic characteristics (age, sex, ethnicity) are more complicated to organize because leadership is not usually clearly defined. If the campaign organization names one person to head a group, it has to be careful that it is not stepping into a factional situation which could drive supporters of another faction into the arms of the other candidate. This was particularly a problem in the Alexander campaign when it came to organizing blacks. The issue was resolved by not naming anyone to a statewide position; instead, local coordinators were appointed. Factionalism is less of a problem when it comes to organizing groups that are themselves less coherent — youth, women (sometimes), and senior citizens.

In Massachusetts, the Sargent campaign made a serious effort to organize identifiable support for the governor from the liberal constituencies in the state. For the campaign staff, it was

---

[15]J. David Greenstone, *Labor in American Politics* (New York: Alfred A. Knopf, 1969).

a question of gaining access to the lists of appropriate organizations and soliciting support from the membership, at the same time getting recognized leaders within the liberal community to endorse Sargent publicly. Typically, the liberal leadership was unable to agree upon a single endorsement statement, so each leader made his or her own.

In order to demonstrate the support such groups give the campaign — which is their reason for being in the first place — the groups may meet occasionally, pay for newspaper or radio and television ads expressing their interest, and solicit their friends for contributions to the campaign. They exist in order to draw attention to the candidate and his or her positions vis-à-vis themselves. A good example of the publicity these groups can achieve was a letter to the editor written by Harry Weger, head of Indiana's muzzle-loading association and treasurer of "Hoosiers for the Truth about Gun Control" — a Bayh campaign special group. The letter, published in a number of newspapers around the state, drew attention to the opponent's past position on gun control, which appeared to be at variance with the Republican campaign position. Weger's argument on Bayh's behalf was much stronger than any argument Bayh might have made for himself, particularly because Weger was already known throughout the state to those interested in guns.

Clerical Work

Clerical work, while routine, requires considerable organization to accomplish. An unbalanced work flow will be felt far more than in the less measurable areas of organizing in the field or doing research (assuming, in this instance, that research is a solitary task, not dependent upon others for its accomplishment).

As temporary organizations that are highly task oriented, political campaigns are neither hierarchical nor bureaucratic. The interaction between members of the organization is usually intense and informal because people spend so much of their waking hours in the campaign headquarters. The intensity and the informality notwithstanding, there was still a considerable distance seen between the professionals (by which I mean here anyone not engaged in a clerical task) and the clerical workers. The result of the distance was two separate lines of communication in the organization, and two separate value systems about the work.

Although the professionals tended to be young, low paid, and politically motivated, the clerical workers were not always so young, nor necessarily low paid, nor so politically involved.[16] When there were differences, there were conflicts. When the clerical workers were young (and often when they were single) they tended to be included more in the informal organizational activities and to be more caught up in the general flow of information and attitudes. It is also true that the professionals tended to be male and the clerical workers female, though there were exceptions.

The most obvious difference was alignment by gender. Even when there were women in the professional group, they tended to have closer relations with the women in the clerical group; and men in the clerical group tended to identify themselves with men in the professional group. As is true of almost everything that can be said of campaigns, this double world exists in most other organizations as well. In many ways it may be less exaggerated in campaigns than it is in permanent organizations because of the informality and intensity of the experience, but the consequences may be more severe for campaigns because they are temporary organizations and have fewer resources or opportunities to compensate.

Part of the difference in attitude was related to the difference in rewards: those at the bottom of a hierarchy, whose work patterns are completely determined by others above them, are the ones to feel the least sense of gratification. Whether or not this is absolutely true of the most hierarchical bureaucratic structures, it was certainly true that, in all three campaigns

---

[16]The secretary to the director of the field organization in Massachusetts was paid $225 per week, in contrast to the salary of $70 per week paid to several of the in-house coordinators on the staff. The salary differential reflected the fact that she was on leave from a state agency and that she had a child to support, while the professionals on the staff were single and came from outside the state bureaucracy.

studied, those with responsibility for the production of other people's work felt that those others were inefficient, egotistical, and generally lacking in perception. As one of the secretaries in Tennessee described it, "The men in the office have a different philosophy of life. They have to have a real driving force behind them. The job comes first and everything else second. They expect to work ten or twelve hours a day. I'm ready to go home after eight or nine hours and put my work behind me. With these different philosophies it's hard to understand them. Everything has to be done right now. If it does not get done until next week. . . . Well, we take their urgent priorities with a grain of salt."

Taking those "urgent priorities with a grain of salt" resulted in a perhaps unconscious, but certainly consistent delay in the work. To the secretaries who felt this way, the campaign was something like a yardstick with numbers at one end — the end that demanded 3,000 copies of something immediately. But there were no measures at the other end of the stick, if the work was not completed until two or three days later. There were no repercussions.

Probably the reason there were no repercussions is related to the uncertain environment. People prove their worth to the organization by their ability to get any given job done. If the job takes longer than expected (because the secretaries took longer than was hoped), anyone with a little imagination can still prove his worth by explaining why it is important that these 3,000 copies of X go out Wednesday, thirteen days before the election, rather than Friday, eighteen days before the vote — if it goes out Friday it will arrive Monday and be lost in the heavy mail that always comes in after the weekend; people will forget so far in advance; if it comes in the middle of the week, people will have time to talk it over with their associates at the office when they are already bored by office work. . . .

Usually the delay in work was unconscious, or if conscious it was passive. In some cases it was construed as a battle with winners and losers: "If you're strong enough to stand the gaff you can win, and you can force mistakes by other people by doing your job. You can win by forcing others to make mistakes."

The fact that the people who expressed anger and frustration were female may have something to do with their unaggressive behavior. The women in clerical positions were in sex-typed jobs, and although a number of them expressed frustration with their jobs and hoped to get into professional fields, as a group their defenses were passive and in keeping with traditional social behavior for women. Those who were the least passive were younger and less socialized in traditional norms.

In some cases there was no conflict between the goals of the professionals and the goals of the clerical staff. This was usually (though not always) the case when the two groups were compatible in age and marital status and shared a common social life. In Tennessee, particularly, a number of the secretaries were married with family responsibilities and just coming back to the labor market. The campaign was a job, almost like any other job, and because they were not politically oriented, they derived fewer rewards in either job satisfaction or expectation of future returns for their work. The young single secretaries, in contrast, though not necessarily more politically involved, felt no other demands on their time and were more socially involved with the single males on the staff.

Chapter 5

The Organization as a Campaign

This chapter is about those aspects of the campaign that draw public attention to the candidate and to the meaning of the candidacy in the election. Visibility is the purpose of a campaign. How it achieves visibility is partly within and partly beyond its control, because it is outside the scope of the organization, dependent on the unpaid media and the demands put upon it. Although most of the tasks of a campaign are directed toward bringing attention to the candidate, some tasks are specifically concerned with what is said or seen: scheduling, research, speech writing, polling, and the production of paid advertisements and literature.

Although people performing these tasks usually work well together, it is not unusual to find one task group aligned against other task groups of the campaign, particularly when there is some question of priorities, such as the danger of the finance department's accepting contributions from inappropriate sources, or setting up small elite fund-raising dinners that would conflict with the image of an open, people's candidate.

Scheduling

Scheduling decisions probably reflect more accurately what a campaign is all about than anything else, including paid media decisions. Where and with whom candidates appear says a good deal about who they are and what they stand for. Because a candidate's time is a finite and an ever decreasing commodity (the more he or she is used, the more he or she is likely to wear out), those charged with responsibility for achieving the various objectives of the campaign (field organization, fund raising, and media visibility, particularly) must compete with each other for that time.

The outcome of that competition is a mirror of campaign priorities. Birch Bayh, for example, was scheduled into each of the state's media markets with increasing frequency as the campaign went on. His opponent paid much less attention to the media markets outside the Indianapolis area but did spend time addressing civic organizations, such as the Rotary Club. Each strategy probably reflected the expectation of the campaign of where its strength lay: for the Democrats a larger but looser mass support; for the Republicans a smaller but more active middle- and upper-middle-class support.

The scheduling procedure for most campaign staffs is to accept requests from organizations or from their own people in the field and to set up tentative block schedules for the month. The closer one gets to the week or the day, the more detailed the schedule becomes, including the time of day for events, the time it will take to get from one event to another, the names of people who will be traveling with or meeting the candidate at each stop, the telephone numbers of contacts along the route, and so on.

Scheduling criteria include the event itself — how big it will be and who will be there, the timing of the event — whether or not it will fit into the campaign's time frame, and its location — how that relates to the campaign's strategy of high visibility in areas likely to be strongholds. Added to this general list of criteria are campaign task pressures: financial needs that might require the candidate to meet with potential givers, either privately or at fund raisers; the field organization's need for the candidate to charge up the local volunteer organization or soothe ruffled feathers; and the press department's demands that the candidate's exposure in the state media markets be maximized.

Organizational pressures on scheduling decisions are created not only by those within the campaign who compete for the candidate's time, but also by outsiders who want a decision about whether or not the candidate will attend their event. As one of the schedulers in Tennessee described it: "The scheduling department has no way of knowing what's important, and we can write off events through naiveté. County people will call up and tell you lies because they want what they want." Put another way by the lieutenant governor of Massachusetts: "People believe that what they are doing is *the* most important thing — to them, the whole election will turn on whether or not the candidate gets into their whistle stop."[1]

For the campaign organization the problem is exacerbated by the desire to keep some flexibility in the schedule so as to allow the candidate to respond to late-breaking events or accept what might prove a more important engagement, and by the uncertainty of not being able to evaluate the worth to the campaign of competing events. Incumbents have some advantage in coping with the latter problem because they can substitute tradition for other criteria in the face of uncertainty. This was particularly true in the Bayh campaign, where the scheduler had the advantage of past campaigns to draw upon and the strong party activities that were a tradition in themselves.

The need for flexibility made the decision-making process in Tennessee particularly difficult during the course of the study

---

[1]Interview with Sally Montgomery, Tennessee scheduler, September 23, 1974, and Massachusetts Lieutenant Governor Donald Dwight, November 7, 1974.

because the candidate was stressing his desire to appear on the same platform as his opponent. For him to be available to travel around the state at a moment's notice, the schedulers had to keep events tentative far longer than was usually the case. Ordinarily, the Alexander campaign preferred to "firm up" the schedule ten days in advance. By not doing so, they lost at least one event in late September because the local planners felt they were deprived of the time necessary to get out the publicity to draw a crowd. The tendency to suboptimize at the local level notwithstanding, the problems of local planners were quite real, and they certainly were not helped by last-minute decision making.

It is one thing to make a decision to go through with an event at the last minute, and it is quite another to make a last-minute decision to cancel an appearance — which is one reason why schedulers prefer to keep things tentative. When they do have to cancel, however, the burden falls on the schedulers to do so in a way that will not be politically costly to the candidate. Obviously, some reasons are more acceptable than others: pressing national or local events, such as an important vote in the Senate or the busing crisis in Boston are acceptable (though there were some expressions of parochialism directed at the campaign headquarters by people in the field who were not touched by what was going on in the Boston schools). Birch Bayh had to cancel a number of stops during the first week of the study because he had the flu and, given the heavy nature of his schedule, he was having a hard time shaking it.

Although there is a tendency to view the candidate more like a distributable good than a human being, the tremendous amount of work that goes into setting up an event (often including political trade-offs of one form or another at the local level) makes cancellation hard to bear. This is especially true if it is the only activity planned by a particular organization or community to include the candidate. Not only are the original costs of time, energy, and politicking lost, but there is also the loss of expected benefits, most notably the opportunity to impress the candidate with the potential of local talent.

Because of such pressures from the campaign staff and outsiders, making decisions on scheduling is often a frustrating process. In almost every other sector of campaign activity, the resources do not compete as directly as they do in scheduling. If one wants $500 to print and distribute a piece of literature, for example, there are many alternative procedures: one can reallocate resources in one's own budget, appeal to the general fund for more money, lower one's expectations and spend half or a quarter of the orginal sum, or try to raise the money elsewhere and have it earmarked for the literature. There is, however, only one candidate, and even though the campaign may be able to send a surrogate speaker (members of the candidate's family or other important political or social figures), surrogates are usually little compensation for the real thing. (There are, of course, occasions when the surrogate is more sought after than the candidate — such as when a particularly charismatic national figure comes in to help out a local campaign — but that does not necessarily change the nature of the competition; it only replaces the central figure.)

Usually, campaigns try to alleviate the chaos that scheduling decisions can create by limiting the number of participants in the process. This seemed to be most effective in the Bayh campaign, where the organization was helped by the incumbency. Not only are there traditions in Indiana about where a candidate appears, there is also a system in the organization, which has grown up during Bayh's twelve years in office. It is the advantage of a permanent organization over a temporary one. In this case, the scheduler and her assistant worked with the head of the field organization (who had most say on political appearances), with the press secretary (who was assured one media event a day, which his office advanced with the local coordinators), and with the finance department. Regional coordinators were expected to press their interests with her, but only a few did, including the coordinator of Marion County, who had an office only a few feet away from the scheduling office. The scheduler usually spoke at least once a day with the senator, who stated his preferences and often made specific requests about events. If there was any dispute among the staff, the decision was to be settled by the administrative assistant.

The process, of course, was not quite as neat as this outline suggests, because staff members would press their suit with Bayh directly and there were occasions when the staff wanted to do one thing and the senator another. Such differences usually came about when the staff wanted to change a traditional activity (such as telephone call-in shows during the last week of the campaign) or when the candidate saw his opponent doing something different, such as attending Rotary meetings. Both those circumstances reflected the uncertainty of campaign decision making.

Another factor in the tensions that decision making on schedules evokes is what stage the campaign is in. The frustration evident in Tennessee was at least partly due to the fact that the study was undertaken during the last half of September, when the campaign objectives were still to be met and proponents of each activity were not willing to see their events unattended by the candidate. The people concerned about the field organization felt they were getting short shrift by the delays. The campaign manager resolved the problem by saying he needed to settle the finance dinners: once fund raising was taken care of, everything else would fall into place.

By the time the study was undertaken in Indiana (the first half of October), the demands of the press department had been worked out. Furthermore, because the fund-raising program was premised on the assumption that the senator would be unavailable for most of the campaign (attending the expected impeachment trial in Washington), there was not much conflict from that quarter. The field organization was the only major call on his time.

Massachusetts had a different situation altogether. There were, in effect, three separate scheduling operations and two separate campaign organizations. Communication was difficult at best. When it was decided by one scheduling section to leave the candidate with some free time, another scheduling section might fill it in. Whereas in Tennessee and Indiana the major campaign objectives were the concern of major departments within the campaign, in Massachusetts only two of the three could be said to be organized enough to provide a center of energy to press their needs: field organization and media. Finance was too splintered, and no representative from that group was found in the upper echelons where campaign decisions were made, at least not during the last few weeks of the campaign when the study was undertaken. The uneven distribution of influence in the Sargent campaign added to the tendency of the organization to make ad hoc decisions, and scheduling decisions were as likely as any to fall within that category, within the limits of the one external determinant — the weekly televised debates with the opposition. There was an additional pressure on the Massachusetts scheduling process that was not seriously felt in the other races, though it did occasionally come up in Indiana: the incumbency of the candidate. As the sitting governor of the state, Sargent believed he should be available for decision making as the state's chief executive, particularly during the busing crisis.

Along with the need to find a balance among the major campaign objectives, another pressure upon scheduling comes from the candidate himself or from those who travel with him in the "road show," who advocate his interests. While those in the campaign headquarters are clamoring for more of the candidate's time, the road show people often argue for more free time to enable him to rest, to perform the less obvious chores such as telephoning, and so on. As one candidate put it when asking for a lighter schedule, "It's not just the hours, it's being on stage all the time."

In each of the three campaigns, the road show consisted of two relatively young men who traveled with the candidate. One of them performed press functions; the other acted as a general aide, transmitting messages, listening to complaints, keeping the candidate informed about matters back at headquarters, as well as briefing him on the people and the important issues at each stop. Another road show function was more personal: alleviating some of the loneliness of campaigning, criticizing the candidate's performance, and keeping up a positive spirit about the whole thing.

Having access is one of the most important factors in politics, and no one has more access to the candidate than his road show companions. Their influence can be considerable. Their value lies in their ability to differentiate the important from the unimportant and to report accurately the nature of problems within the organization, as well as with the campaign at large. Still, it must have been strange for these candidates to spend almost all their waking hours in the company of young men many years their junior (less true in Tennessee because of the youth of the candidate). Bayh's road show duo were twenty years younger; Sargent's closer to thirty-five years younger. The value of their youth was the energy and enthusiasm they brought to their tasks; the drawbacks were less obvious, perhaps adding to the loneliness that can be felt by the more sensitive candidate.

Research

There are three kinds of political research: gathering information and taking positions on issues; acquiring background information on each locality the candidate is likely to visit during the course of a campaign; and gathering information about the opposition — his or her record, current positions, and relevant information on background, sometimes known as the "negative research." For many people, political research is the most interesting activity of a campaign; and although campaigns usually have a few full-time staff members in charge of research activities, it is not at all uncommon to find a wide array of volunteers engaged in research activity of one sort or another.

Issue Research

Most campaigns have three or four important issues on which the candidates disagree and which are generally acknowledged to be what the election is all about. These issues, or themes, are straightforward and known early in the campaign. Occasionally, new evidence will turn up in the course of the campaign to add greater weight to a position, but on the whole the candidate travels around the state repeating himself on the major campaign themes. Most of the issue research that goes on during the course of the campaign, therefore, tends to be about less significant matters, often responses to external events or to direct questions asked of the candidate by groups and individuals. The most valuable research is that which will enable the candidate to win press coverage and appear on the evening news.

Research and press departments usually work closely together, because the work of the research department will most effectively appear as a speech, a campaign press release, or a media event.

Although the volunteers who offer to do research might be seen as a new resource of great value in uncovering old scandals or new solutions to current problems, it rarely happens that way. As the head of the research department in Indiana noted, "At one point I had organized a group of young attorneys to do research in Indianapolis, but it had mixed results — about a 50 percent success rate. Some people worked very hard, but were of no help. They might turn in a treatise on mass transit which we couldn't use. But the biggest problem was people not doing it. They would come back with a half-baked job and we would just do it ourselves. I found two or three guys that would do good work whom we would rely on and I ended up using just them."[2] The head of the research department in Tennessee had a similar experience. Both had looked for young attorneys or law students.

It is not insignificant that the policy or research heads of all three campaigns were lawyers or law students and that they assigned research tasks primarily to members of their profession. The other major category of campaign researchers is academic (either students or faculty). Both groups tend to work on a project basis. Presumably both groups are adept at identifying the salient elements of a problem and are trained to write. Probably the most significant similarity is the tendency for those groups to see themselves either as being issue oriented, if not ideological, or as having a sense of public duty.

In all three campaigns there was a tendency for the people who worked on issues to differentiate themselves from the rest of the campaign staff, sometimes in a way that produced organizational tension (particularly in Tennessee and Massachusetts). Issues tend to create categories of adherents who take sides. Although partisan politics is premised on there being several sides, *within* a party there is a sense of the need for compromise in order to maintain organizational solidarity.

---

[2]Interview with Thomas Connaughton, Indiana research director, October 2, 1974.

Party unity notwithstanding, it is not uncommon for the issue people to be wary of the political people in the same organization, lest their positions be "sold out."

Such division was most obvious in Tennessee, where the issue people had a sign on their door calling themselves "the left wing." Meant originally as a joke in the primary, it was reflective of the concerns expressed by the issue people that others in more traditional tasks (particularly in finance) would deflect the campaign from its important theme of openness about campaign contributions.

In Massachusetts, the issue people were a major faction in the statehouse organization, and although the head of the policy staff viewed himself primarily as a politician, his loyal adherents were more inclined to believe in good and evil — with evil on the other side. Most of the policy staff was so focused on the need to overcome opposition to their views that they paid relatively little attention to the campaign organization.

In Indiana, the research department worked closely with the press department (which was alienated from the rest of the staff for its own reasons) and seemed on the whole less aligned than its counterparts in the other two campaigns. This may have been due in large measure to the permanent nature of the organization and the relatively small size of a Senate staff. A Senate office usually consists of a small number of rooms with a large number of desks squeezed in to accommodate the staff. The physical closeness is not conducive to distant working relations, and most people have a fair idea of what others on the staff are doing. Normally a campaign evokes a sense of isolation and uncertainty as to what others are doing. The permanence of the Bayh staff appears to have alleviated some of that distance and isolation, at least between the research and the political departments, though it was probably equally important that both departments were located near each other.

Political issue research is a somewhat specialized field. It calls for an analysis of the issue in a form that can be easily translated into a speech, a press release, or a one-page handout, to say nothing of a media event or a campaign ad. It must enable candidates to differentiate themselves from their opponents, by taking a different view of the problem, by offering a different solution, or by breaking new ground altogether and calling attention to a problem that had not heretofore been considered a campaign issue. The last is usually difficult to accomplish in a campaign, because there is a tendency on the part of voters to assume that anything a candidate says during the campaign period is done only to attract attention — an assumption not without some merit — and hence it is harder to establish new issues. In 1972, for example, George McGovern tried to establish corruption as an issue because of the Watergate break-in, but the only issue that seemed to elicit serious support was his already known position against the war. In the Sargent campaign, the press was able to generate interest in the question of whether or not Mrs. Sargent made an illegal loan to the campaign, but the issue lost credibility when the opposition tried to use it as evidence of Sargent's corruption. Because of the difficulty of establishing new priorities, the most that issue research can normally do is allow the candidate to participate in a dramatization (a visual presentation) of current events.

Because research is an individual activity, almost any number can participate, each one believing he or she is making a substantial contribution to the campaign. Assigning volunteers to do research is a solution to the perennial campaign problem of finding something rewarding for people to do — particularly for people who believe they have a substantial contribution to offer the campaign in terms of their training or general level of intelligence. Nor need one be disappointed if the research does not result in a press conference the day after it is turned in. It might become a big issue the next day, or it might be used in another part of the state, or saved for the right moment, or used once the candidate is safely in office. The research staff may be frustrated because they hoped for something more immediately useful, but they need not let their disappointment show and risk alienating the volunteer who is, if nothing else, a supporter. Using volunteers to do campaign research may be wasteful, but it is not organizationally dysfunctional.

Background Research

Background research, although performed by the same people who research issues, is less likely to cause organizational dissension. In most cases, the researcher will rely fairly heavily on the political people for a sense of what the salient issues are in a community, including a knowledge of how local leaders get on with one another. If the candidate is an incumbent, it is also important to know what he or she might have said before in the community — particularly if there were any promises made to help solve local problems.

Background research also requires a close relationship with the campaign scheduler in order to know where the candidate is going and what kind of information will be required. Needless to say, if there is confusion about what the candidate is going to do it makes the task of the background researcher more difficult, and bad feelings can develop between research and scheduling because of it.

Once the background research is done it is often put into a looseleaf notebook and given to the candidate or an aide who travels with him on the road show. The book in Tennessee included the day's schedule; a county profile of each of the counties Alexander would visit on a given day, including a political breakdown of the voting record; any issue material he might need in relation to a specific event; copies of all the press releases for that week; a prepared speech (if needed); and a copy of the long-range block schedule.

Negative Research

Although campaigns always assign someone to research the background of the opponent, that is usually a relatively minor activity in terms of the deployment of the research department's resources. There is some variation from campaign to campaign in the energy devoted to negative research, depending on whether or not the opponent is an incumbent or has held public office before. There may also be a difference if the campaign looks as if it is losing, in which case the negative research may feed into negative ads (though the choice of whether or not to run a negative campaign is not totally dictated by the standing in the polls). In fact, it is often surprising but always true that even if a candidate has a low standing in the polls, the campaign organization tends to believe in ultimate victory.

The tactics of the Committee to Re-Elect the President in 1972 notwithstanding, negative research is usually drawn from public records, not from engaging in undercover activity. Those records might include newspaper clippings, published hearings in which the opponent had a part, inconsistencies in his campaign statements, and so on. It often happens that someone out in the field will volunteer damaging information about the opposition, but the campaign organization tends to view these gifts with some suspicion. Should they not be provable, or should the information be altogether wrong, charges may backfire. Charges can backfire, in fact, even when the information is correct and verifiable because they may well smack of dirty politics.

Another reason why negative research and a good portion of positive research never gets used has to do with the nature of campaigning. Much of the paper that is turned in does not get read by those who make the decisions about what to say: the candidate and the top aides. The press of activity is great, making reading something of a luxury, and decisions are made on such an ad hoc basis that unless the researcher or someone who read the report is in the room when the decision is made, it may not even get a hearing.

Needless to say, should the research turn up something that appears vital to the campaign it will be given attention. Most of what is said in the course of campaigning, however, is superficial — variations on a simple theme. Otherwise, research gets turned into speeches, campaign literature, or position papers that are available upon request, usually from academics.

Speech Writing

Formal speeches are a surprisingly small part of day-to-day campaigning. Even when the candidate is called upon to address a sit-down occasion such as a lunch or dinner meeting, the tendency is to present off-the-cuff remarks that reflect what the candidate has been saying during the campaign in general or that day in particular. There is, after all, a value in appearing spontaneous. A speech is generally prepared when the audience is interested in a specific issue, when the occasion is formal (and likely to attract media attention), or when close attention will be paid to what the candidate says, as in the case of a debate. It was only in Massachusetts, where the candidate had a series of televised debates with his opponent, that speech writing was an important part of the campaign.

Perhaps the most important reason speeches are seldom written is that whenever the candidate has an opportunity to make a speech, he stresses the important themes of his campaign, and after a little experience the phrases he uses to express those themes come to mind as easily as his name and address do. On the one hand, the candidate's function is to explain why he or she ought to be elected, and hence the repetition of themes, but on the other hand, too much repetition makes the candidate appear unspontaneous if not bored. This is also a problem for the press following a candidate. It accounts for the tendency of the media to focus on peripheral happenings on the campaign trail. In any case, the need to repeat the major themes, and the facility the candidate develops to do so independently, account for the small role speech writers have in a statewide campaign.

Speech writing is a sensitive art, requiring the writer to be able to catch the speech patterns of the subject and to create phrases that seem natural to both the speaker and the listener. It is a question of cadence, intonation, and style. It also requires an ability to translate an issue into a message of compassion, strength, and interest. Writing a speech undoubtedly comes more easily in those situations where there is a close relationship between the writer and the speaker (unless the writer is particularly talented or experienced, which is more likely to be the case in a presidential campaign). Learning to write a speech is only part of the process: the speaker must also learn to work with the writer and must be able to deliver the speech. The temporary nature of a campaign organization is not conducive to the development of that kind of relationship, though a more permanent governor's staff is and to a lesser extent (lesser because it is smaller) so is a Senate staff.

The greater importance, therefore, of speeches in the Sargent campaign was partly a result of the focus on televised debates, and partly a result of having available the resources of a staff that had worked with the candidate for many years. The Bayh campaign had some of that organizational skill, but the person on the staff designated as the speech writer was relatively new to the organization and did not feel he had a strong enough sense of Senator Bayh's style to write well for him. In contrast to those incumbent organizations, the Alexander campaign had neither the organizational resources to employ a speech writer nor a candidate experienced at relying on others to write for him.

Although speech writing is a solitary task — as is most of the work in research — the opportunity for organizational conflict can arise when there are several people working on drafts. The pattern among the Massachusetts statehouse staff was for there to be discussion with the top aides and the governor on what direction the speech should take: its tone, the issues to be raised. Following that, two and possibly three or four drafts would be prepared by as many people. A second meeting would be held when each of the drafts would be criticized, and the speech would be given either to Jack Flannery, Sargent's chief secretary and closest aide, to rewrite, or first to Al Kramer, the policy chief, and then to Flannery. As Flannery noted, the best way to get a speech through would be to hand it to the governor thirty minutes before he was due to deliver it and explain that there was not even time to retype it.

Polling

Polling is either done under the aegis of the research department through the use of volunteers or contracted out to a professional political polling organization. In recent years it has become one of the most important tools a campaign organization uses to alleviate uncertainty. Polls have important consequences for the organization in helping it decide how to allocate its resources: where to deploy volunteers, schedule the candidate, and use the media. Another value polling has for a campaign is in fund raising: "Giving some credibility to the candidate and showing his or her potential, especially when the candidate is not an incumbent." If victory can be predicted by something as concrete as a poll, it is a strong incentive to many would-be donors who want to be on the winning side. This is especially true in recent years with the advent of public disclosure of contributions. The political pollster is also available to the campaign for press conferences, which were described by one pollster as the opportunity to "be exploited by your client."

Although the greatest value of the poll for the campaign is in alleviating uncertainty by measuring voter concern and motivation, the secondary benefit of measuring the strength of the candidate vis-à-vis the opposition is the one everyone looks to — the press, the campaign organization, the candidate, and potential campaign contributors. When there are several polls showing conflicting results about who is ahead and how far, as there were in Massachusetts, the uncertainty increases.

Polling can take several forms: in-depth interviewing of a carefully selected sample (one professional polling organization usually does 400 such interviews in a statewide race, costing $20 per interview — somewhere between $8,000 and $12,000 per poll); telephone interviews (costing $10 per interview); or shopping center interviews (usually with volunteers). It is not unusual for a campaign to spend around $20,000 for polling, beginning with in-depth interviews in the early stages of the campaign and proceeding to secondary polling later with telephone interviews. The value of early polling is obvious if the campaign is going to use the results in allocating resources. Secondary polling is helpful in testing the effects of the campaign when voters have had an opportunity to consider the candidates more fully.[3]

The styles and consequences of polling were different for each of the three campaigns, probably revealing the range of possible effects. In Tennessee, an early poll by a professional pollster showed the candidate far behind, but much of the support for the opposition was "soft," which is to say it could erode and swing to Alexander's side. The staff kept the poll secret lest it hinder their fund-raising effort, but they did run shopping center polls on weekends, from which they claimed

---

[3]Interview with Dorothea Lynch, senior analyst, Cambridge Survey Research Corporation, May 8, 1975.

they were able to measure progress: usually an increase of 1.5 to 2 percentage points a week. The opposition campaign, however, held a press conference in mid-September to enable its pollster to make public his findings, showing Blanton considerably ahead (figures that corresponded with Alexander's private poll), giving a morale boost to Blanton's campaign and acting as something of a depressent on the Alexander staff even though they publicly debunked that poll.

The Bayh campaign made the most sophisticated use of polling, employing not only an external political polling organization but also its own in-house pollster, who did further analyses of the outside pollster's data as well as telephone polling of her own several times during the course of the campaign. The greater dependence of the Indiana campaign on polling was due in large measure to the history of the Bayh organization in trying to apply computer technology to politics, an effort that went back before the 1968 campaign.[4]

Polling may help a campaign address itself to issues because it clarifies what issues are of concern to the voting population, and which groups among that population are likely to be supportive of the candidate. The Bayh people knew from their polling that those who thought of Birch Bayh as a big spender (which was the early thrust of the Lugar campaign against Bayh) would tend to vote against him. Those who did not think him a big spender would support him.[5] The Bayh campaign was also able to measure voter opinion on abortion reform in the course of the campaign: with the exception of a very small portion of the electorate, most voters either favored liberal reforms or did not intend to cast their ballots because of a candidate's stand one way or the other on the issue. Although

---

[4]John Dibble, untitled paper on the Bayh organization (Columbia University, 1968).

[5]Campaign issues can also include the relative virtues of the personalities of the candidates, particularly when the office sought is an executive office such as governor or president. It is probably not irrelevant that Sargent seemed open and appeared to have a sense of humor and his opponent seemed closed and arrogant. According to the head of the Bayh field organization, David Bochnowski, their polls showed that Indiana voters identified with Bayh's personality, not with issue positions he had taken.

abortion had been one of the campaign issues, and although the Bayh headquarters was besieged by a right-to-life petition campaign, the organization was able to drop the issue, responding to it only in those areas where opposition was particularly well organized.

Although most of the emphasis in the Bayh polling was related to issues and how the organization might respond to issue preferences, there were some organizational consequences of the data showing him to be in the lead. The campaign was having trouble raising money, as were the other two campaigns studied, and chose to save money by buying less media time for ads. According to one of the decision makers, they would not have risked going off the air if they were not ahead in the polls. They also probably would not have risked it if Bayh were not an incumbent with such high name recognition in the state.

It would be misleading to assume that polling alleviates all of the uncertainty. The pollster's data comprise only one input in the campaign's decision process. Others include the technological sophistication of the decision makers and their attitude about accepting the data, the political strength within the organization of various issue advocates, and the opportunity for the candidate to take action on any given issue. In the McGovern campaign in 1972, for example, the polling data showed the same results on abortion that the Bayh data showed in 1974, but the campaign's decision makers could not bring themselves to believe it and act accordingly. If the candidate is an incumbent or has previously held public office, he or she may also be bound by positions and alliances taken and made in the past.

Perhaps the clearest example of polls *creating* uncertainty was in the Massachusetts campaign when the state's leading newspaper, *The Boston Globe,* published a poll in mid-October showing the incumbent trailing his opponent by 25 points. The Sargent campaign had taken a poll of its own, at almost the same time as the *Globe's* poll, which showed him trailing by only 10 points. The difference was significant, especially because the election was only three weeks away. Not only was the *Globe* poll a depressant on the campaign organization as a whole, but it also affected the campaign's fund raising and it occupied the time of the campaign decision makers for several days, as they tried to understand the reason for the difference between the polls and to do something about it.

It was easier in Tennessee for the Alexander people to openly debunk the Blanton poll because that was, after all, the work of the opposition. The *Globe*, though thought to be leaning toward Dukakis (erroneously, as it happened, because the newspaper endorsed Sargent a few days before the election), could not be accused of playing politics. It was presumably an objective observer, though the publication of the poll created considerable discussion among the newspaper's readers of the appropriateness of a newspaper, whose function was to report the news, getting into the business of making news and having an impact on the outcome of events.

In the end, the campaign organization decided not to hire an independent pollster to do a third poll (at an additional cost of $15,000), and not to waste more time than had already been spent trying to understand the explanations offered by both the campaign's pollster and the newspaper's pollster for the difference in their results. Their was nothing the organization could or would do differently in any case.

Given the uncertainty and anxiety generated by the poll in mid-October, the newspaper was more cautious with its pre-election poll, traditionally published on the Sunday before election day. The pollster kept his interviewers in the field an extra day because they were finding too great a flux in the response, and the findings were not published until the day before the election. They showed Sargent trailing Dukakis by only 6 points.

It is interesting to note that the narrowed margin was greeted with great enthusiasm by the campaign organization, which believed it was going to win after all. A neutral observer might have been less heartened by the results, but campaign intensity and excitement can overcome almost any external negative sign. It was argued, for example, that if there is a 5 percent chance for error, if the poll erred in Dukakis' favor, and if the flux in the field was indicative of a change of voter favor from Dukakis to Sargent, then the one percentage point that Sargent was actually behind on Saturday (subtracting the margin for error) would be overcome by Tuesday.

The greatest value of polling in alleviating uncertainty is in the area of issues and voter motivation. These are complex elements and there are rarely competing polls available with which to compare the results. When it comes to predicting the outcome of the election — a valuable tool for the campaign that it can show itself to be a winner — there is a danger of adding to rather than alleviating the uncertainty if other pollsters show other results. As one Sargent aide noted, "We are currently being victimized by conflicting polls and we are paying too much attention to them and the mood changes in relation to them." Still, it is hard to give up looking to the polls because the desire to predict the future is very compelling. When, a few days later, a radio call-in show conducted a poll and found Sargent favored over Dukakis 21 to 9, campaign spirits soared again, even though everyone knew the worthlessness of that kind of self-selected sample.

Paid Media Advertising

The objective for both paid and unpaid campaign media advertising is to present the candidate in the best possible light. Clearly there is more control over the paid media in achieving that objective. Whether the paid media campaign is positive (describing the virtues of the candidate) or negative (attacking the opposition), it does try to present a theme that will be repeated in other areas of campaign activity. In Indiana, for example, a major theme of the campaign was that Birch Bayh was "one man who makes a difference." It was designed to take advantage of his incumbency in the Senate and to enable the campaign to point to his accomplishments. It was used on posters and the literature the campaign gave out.

Whether or not a campaign chooses a positive or a negative media approach will depend on several factors: the preferences and experience of the professional producers, the candidate, and the staff; the closeness of the race; and the circumstances of the campaign, which is to say the particular political traditions in the state and the activity of the opposition. Sometimes the strategy will change during the course of the campaign, and although there is usually considerable latitude in what an agency will do, it has been known to happen that a campaign will go to another agency to produce a different kind of ad.[6] One reason this seldom happens is the difficulty of finding another agency at the last minute, but more important reasons are the heavy commitment in money and the contractual relationship the campaign organization establishes with the media producers.

Of the three campaigns, two contracted their media production to outside agencies: the Alexander campaign to an agency in another city, the Sargent campaign to one in another state. The Bayh campaign, although hiring an outside agency for its basic production facilities, did its own editing and kept control over the decisions. Because the Bayh campaign was hard pressed for money and generally not pleased with the production quality of the outside agency, it delayed payment until the end of the campaign. As a result, it could not gain access to film footage on the candidate held by the out-of-state agency and was restricted in its ability to shift the focus of the media campaign midway. In contrast, the Sargent campaign had strained but constant interaction with its media producers and was able to produce ads late in the campaign that reflected last-minute strategies.

Another function of the advertising agency, aside from the production of radio and television ads, is the placement of those ads with local stations. In Tennessee and Massachusetts, the agency performed both tasks; in Indiana, an advertising agency in the state bought time for the campaign. One reason for going through the agency is that it has time buyers on its staff who are familiar with the varying rates, schedules, and implications of when what is seen where. Another reason is that stations pay the agencies a fee — usually 15 percent. If a campaign organization buys time directly from the station, the

---

[6]In the latter days of the 1972 presidential campaign, the McGovern organization chose to find another producer of paid media advertisements because Charles Guggenheim, their major media producer, did not believe in the effectiveness of negative advertising. Noted in Ernest May and Janet Fraser, eds., *Campaign '72: The Managers Speak* (Cambridge: Harvard University Press, 1973), 212.

stations keep that 15 percent and thus the campaign saves no money. Buying time for a statewide campaign is also a complicated bookkeeping process with which the temporary campaign organization is ill equipped to deal.

There are strategies in buying time. Advertising people bring some professional skills to this task. They know, for example, when an audience is most likely to be attentive ("drive time" — the rush hours, when people are stuck in their cars with few distractions besides their radios — is one example; others include time before, during, and after evening news shows on television, and so on); what kind of audience a particular station or show attracts (young voters in Massachusetts, for example, were shown in the polls to be inclined to support the opposition, so placing ads on radio stations that played rock music and appealed to young audiences was probably not the best use of campaign resources); and which stations or shows were likely to reach the largest audiences. In Indiana, the time buyer for the Democratic party decided to place party ads during the first half of Indiana University football games, under the theory that the team was so bad no one would bother listening to the second half. The cost of the time reflects the value that buyers place on the size and nature of the audience.

Another factor in time buying is the location of the audience. A high proportion of the Democratic vote in Indiana lives in the Lake County area, just outside of Chicago. To buy time on the television stations in Chicago would be an expensive proposition because of the size of the audience, and also because most of that audience lives in Illinois. It would be a waste of campaign resources. For that reason, the Bayh campaigners focused their media effort in that area on radio because radio is cheaper and its audience more localized.

Strategies are not the only issue when it comes to buying time; consideration must also be given to what the stations are willing to sell. This is a problem not only because station managements might have political biases (however nonbiased they are supposed to be, according to the FCC), but also because the electronic media are regulated by the federal government and could lose their licenses for unfair political coverage. Usually, this is more a problem for the station than it is for the campaign or its advertising agency, but in Massachusetts it also became a problem for the campaign. Of the three major television stations in the Boston area, one chose not to permit any paid political advertising (offering instead longer free time slots); a second claimed that the campaign filmed an ad from the station's air time and would not run that ad; and the third was afraid it would be liable if Dukakis brought suit against it for carrying an ad that branded him a liar. Part of the problem was due to the negative nature of the campaign's ads, but it was complicated in that what was appropriate from the perspective of the station management differed from that of the campaign and its agency. What is right or wrong in political advertising is not necessarily apparent. It is illegal, for instance, for an unidentified narrator in a political ad to say the opposition lied. It is not illegal for the candidate to say the same of his or her opponent.

The question of whether to run a positive or negative ad, or how strong or soft to make the ad, is one that depends on the temperaments of those involved and the circumstances of the campaign. In Massachusetts the agency had produced an ad it referred to as the "unfair taxes ad." When the decision makers in the campaign saw it, they felt it was too hard-hitting and decided not to let the agency run it. At the time, the campaign pollster had just completed the poll showing the governor 10 points behind Dukakis, a tremendous improvement over its last poll. Feeling that the campaign was narrowing the distance between the two candidates, the Sargent people did not want to risk alienating potential supporters by a hard negative sell. Two days later, *The Boston Globe* published its poll showing Sargent trailing Dukakis by 25 points. Although the campaign staff was unsure of what to do about the difference between the two polls, the possibility that the *Globe* might be right made them decide to let the agency run the "unfair taxes" ad after all, because they would have less to lose and needed to fight with any available tool. There was also a belief among the governor's top advisors that a negative campaign is exciting and necessary for an incumbent; a positive campaign based on Sargent's accomplishments would have been boring.

How successful paid media advertisements are in affecting voter behavior is a moot question. There are those who argue that paid media ads are most effective when neither candidate is well known and one is slightly disliked.[7] Some argue that media ads reinforce already existing attitudes, and the most one can expect is that they will make party identifiers more comfortable about casting their ballots for the party's nominee.[8] What is obvious is that the paid media ads are the most carefully constructed expression of the campaign's intentions and if they are bad they can harm a campaign more seriously than they can help if they are good.

Media strategies are usually developed early in the campaign, but all three organizations studied wanted to reserve their options for last-minute issues. The Bayh campaign staff wanted to use half-hour slots in the last week of the campaign to defend themselves against attacks by a losing opposition. And the incident in Massachusetts with the "unfair taxes" ad underscores the likelihood that a losing candidate will take more chances than a winning candidate who is afraid of alienating supporters.

Literature Production and Distribution

Campaign literature serves two major functions: it adds to the campaign's visibility by explaining in more detail than the media ads do what the campaign is about, who the candidate is, and what the positions are on important issues; and more important for the organization, its distribution provides a task for the volunteers in the field. Receiving something as tangible as a piece of paper may also have some effect on the voter's tendency to vote for a candidate, although there is no proof of this. Basically, campaigns produce literature because campaigns have always produced literature.

The literature usually includes a general brochure in color on good quality paper with several attractive informal photo-

---

[7]Charles Guggenheim, in May and Fraser, 203.
[8]Walter DeVries and Lance Terrance, *The Ticket Splitters* (Grand Rapids: William B. Eerdmans, 1972).

graphs of the candidate meeting different kinds of people (workers, children, the elderly), the candidate working at his desk with his shirt sleeves rolled up, and usually one or two shots of the candidate with his family. The brochure expresses the theme of the campaign ("Birch Bayh: One Man Who Makes a Difference") and provides a paragraph or two on the issues the organization thinks important in the eyes of the electorate (Bayh's brochure included tax reform, education, and gun control).

Although the Tennessee and Massachusetts campaigns devoted most of their literature production to a general piece, the Indiana campaign spent more of its money and energy in the production of small pamphlets and one-page handouts on specific issues. Because the Bayh campaign was structured in such a way as to elicit voter concerns, the field organization — especially the voter identification program — could be used to direct these issue pieces to those who would have an interest in them and could therefore be most swayed by them. It may also be true that as a Democratic campaign the Bayh organization was made up of the various constituencies reflected in the party's membership, and that there is a tendency to direct specific pieces to specific groups, such as labor, youth, or blacks. Both Republican campaigns were less constituency oriented and tended to present a general image of the candidate, an image that was just as easy to present in a single brochure.

It is interesting to note that, although the general brochures were all professional-looking pieces, the Bayh organization sought to achieve a different objective with their issue literature. The handouts appeared to have been produced with a typewriter and a mimeograph machine and had an amateur look about them. The value of appearing nonprofessional was that it made the piece look more spontaneous and intimate, not as if the campaign were rolling in money — clearly an advantage for those trying to encourage contributions.

The production of the literature is a task usually assigned to the outside ad agency (though such was not the case in Indiana), and for the campaign the more important problem is its availability. As it turned out, this was a serious issue in Tennessee.

The people in charge of the field organization felt they needed to be able to assign tasks to their volunteers to help them feel they were part of an energetic statewide effort. Because the literature (including bumper stickers and campaign buttons) was late in coming, the volunteers in the counties were restless, a situation that could have proved dysfunctional if they chose to go off on their own in attacking the opposition, or if they lost interest in the campaign because there was nothing for them to do.

Chapters Four and Five have focused on what campaign organizations do and on the kinds of issues that confront them as they try to reach out to the voter. Most voter contact with campaigns, however, is not direct. Newspapers have always played an intervening role between the candidate and the electorate. In the past, newspapers were obvious party organs, and partisanship was the raison d'être of any number of publications in America and elsewhere. Their role was to interpret issues, personalities, and events in the light of special interests to which the newspaper appealed.

For a variety of reasons, the clear partisan function of the media has declined, but newspapers, radio, and television still play a major role — most say *the* major intermediary role between the candidate and the voters. The next chapter considers the media and their performance of that role.

Chapter 6

The Campaign and the Media

The news media, especially television, have in the opinion of many seriously weakened the educational and democratic quality of political campaigns. The criticisms of the role of the media are not identical; indeed, they are not always consistent. To some, a candidate and staff manipulate the media by exploiting its technology for their own advantage. Senator Joseph McCarthy in the early 1950s held a sheaf of papers before a television camera and claimed that it was a list of Communists in the State Department — a powerful image that, some feel, launched McCarthy as a national demagogue. To others, however, it is the media that manipulates the campaigns, by selecting what is to be seen and printed and making it impossible for the issues about which the candidates most care to be seriously discussed. A leading example was the news coverage of the protesters outside the 1968 Democratic National Convention in Chicago. To still others, the media neither manipulates nor is manipulated; rather, it trivializes politics by reducing an election to a personality contest, staged with a few simple slogans in order to cater to the shallow entertainment interests of the least sophisticated members of its audience. Finally, some see in the media a persistent bias, leaning systematically to either the political right or left, and making it difficult for centrist candidates to receive fair treatment.

This study cannot analyze seriously or systematically each of those complaints, but it can provide a perspective on them. For one thing, most complaints about the media are heard during or after national contests that the television networks and the national press cover. But most campaigns, obviously, are state and local ones, of only occasional interest to the national media. Although there are clearly some parallels that can be drawn, how the media in these lesser campaigns perform can affect the behavior of thousands of candidates and officeholders. Furthermore, one must compare media coverage of a typical campaign not with some idealized conception of politics as a perfectly educational and democratic process, but with the alternative of a campaign in which the media are unimportant.

The real question is whether there would be greater attention to voter concerns in a campaign where the candidate was presented to the voter solely by means of leaflets, advertisements, and rallies. Though it will doubtless be impossible to make that kind of comparison, it is possible to show — on the basis of a close look at three statewide campaigns — that the effect of the media was, if anything, to broaden the range of issues discussed and to present a fuller perspective on the rival candidates.

The campaign organizations devoted a good deal of their resources to preparing press statements that outnumbered the *different* speeches the candidate gave, to replying to statements made by their rivals in the press, and to developing materials for television ("visuals") that would display the candidate in a favorable light. Whether this was a rational use of the campaign organization's time and resources is open to question.

To understand the role of the media in a campaign, it is first necessary to understand what they cover and why. This, in turn, requires an understanding of the media organizations and their interaction with the campaign organization.

Coverage

Newspaper coverage of campaigns is of three kinds: (1) stories about the campaign based on a press release, issued by the campaign and reprinted almost verbatim; (2) a reporter's stories about an event or an issue, or background pieces, which might include time he or she spent with the candidate; and (3) editorial statements and analyses of the campaign. Sometimes there is continuity in a paper's policy: in Indiana, for example, the Pulliam papers, which were anti-Bayh, seldom gave front-page coverage to the Democratic incumbent, and columns that favored Bayh would rarely appear in them. More often, however, editorial policy did not extend much beyond the editorial page. As one reader of *The Boston Globe*, speaking of the difference between reporters and editors, put it, "You would almost think that there were different organizations at the *Globe*, each with its own parking lot, entrance, and cafeteria."

In all three campaigns the press departments and the candidates spent time with reporters and editorial writers, occasionally submitting themselves to a panel set up by a newspaper that would question the candidate alone or in the company of the opposition. Candidates went through the latter activity in the hope that it would lead to an endorsement, something thought particularly important in Tennessee, where newspaper endorsements were held to be a major factor in the primary victory. Another version of the editorial panel consisted of meetings of the candidate with chapters of Sigma Delta Chi, the journalism fraternity. The press, presumably, comprises a better-informed audience than any other that a candidate might encounter, and there were always careful preparations for these meetings. Except in Massachusetts, no newspaper reporters were assigned to cover the campaign on a regular basis, though the more important papers in the state would send reporters to travel with the candidate for varying periods of time.

Television coverage of campaigns is far more restricted than that of newspapers because of the limits of its technology, the regulations of the Federal Communications Commission (which make it unlikely for a station to endorse a candidate), and the competition of political news with fires and other visually dramatic events that occur each day and must all be fit into a broadcast of a half hour or an hour. A newspaper can, after all, expand the size of the paper to cover the news of the day without losing revenue from advertising. Television news is constricted by time. Some of these limitations are changing with the application of video tape and direct feeds, enabling television stations to broadcast live events occurring during the news program.[1]

Furthermore, although newspaper reporters can easily follow the candidate around the state, television reporters cannot. It is too cumbersome and expensive to fly the cameras, lights, camera crew, and television reporters from Indianapolis to Gary to cover an event, particularly when the Indianapolis station does not reach the Gary viewing area. Consequently, campaigns schedule the candidate on a regular basis (often every two or three days in the last weeks of the campaign) into each of the state's television media markets and plan a "visual" — a filmable event that will be visually interesting to a television audience and that will get a message across about the candidate's position on an issue, by words and by the viewer's recognition of the setting. In order to be filmable, the event will be scheduled in a place where there is either enough light or enough electricity to enable the film crew to plug in their own lights, and enough room to accommodate the press and its equipment. Gas stations and supermarkets are favorite campaign spots as they are technically usable places where the setting will tell much of the story. The visual will occur early enough in the day (no later than mid-afternoon) to allow the station time to develop the film and edit the story for play on the six o'clock news. This will undoubtedly change with the smaller more flexible television equipment now being intro-

---

[1]The equipment is expensive, but it is quite likely that most stations will be so equipped by the end of the 1970s.

duced around the country. Television news departments cover more than scheduled campaign visuals. They also cover press conferences and present stories about the campaign that are read by an anchorman or reporter over a slide of the candidate. Whereas a newspaper may devote several columns a day to a campaign, a half-hour television news show may give it ten seconds to a minute and a half of air time.

Whatever the story is, it will typically be decided upon by the assignment editor in the morning — usually after having read the papers and listened to the radio news reports based on wire service stories, though he too is the recipient of campaign press releases and telephone calls from the campaign press secretary and staff. A reporter and crew will be assigned to cover the candidate at a specific event. On occasion, a reporter may be told to ask a particular question, although there was no instance in this study of much discussion between the reporters and the assignment editor about how a story ought to be covered, or how it might relate to stories on the opposition.

Once a story was filmed, the reporter returned to the studio and edited the processed film. A final decision on whether or not to run the story was made by the producer. In most cases there was little information given or received between the reporter and the news department's production staff other than the time the story should or would take.

The following is a log of what was covered by one television station in each capital city during the period of the study.[2]

Tennessee:

> 9/18 (15 seconds), Wire story — Alexander claims he will get votes from followers of Blanton's primary opponents. No film; slide of Alexander (On the 10 P.M. news, nothing at 6 o'clock.)

> 9/19 (24 seconds) — Alexander repeats his claim to the support of the Democratic losers. One of them denies it. Slide. (On the 6 P.M. news only.)

> 9/20 (12 seconds) — Alexander responding to Blanton's prison reform statement (6 P.M.);

---

[2]Log compiled by Richard Paisner and Richard M. Neustadt.

(15 seconds) — Alexander calling for expansion of mental health centers, from a wire story (10 P.M.).

(No coverage Saturday and Sunday 9/21 and 9/22.)

9/23 (30 seconds) — Alexander reacting to Blanton poll putting Blanton substantially in the lead; film of candidate being interviewed by anchorman (6 and 10 P.M.).

9/24 (14 seconds) — Alexander announces his opposition to expanded strip mining, from wire story (10 P.M., nothing at 6 P.M.).

9/25 (15 seconds) — President Ford may come to Tennessee to campaign for Alexander (both 6 and 10 P.M.).

9/26 (18 seconds) — Alexander in favor of openness in state government, from wire story (shown at 10, nothing at 6 P.M.).

9/27 (1 minute) — Film from Knoxville of Alexander and Blanton at a joint appearance (shown at 6, nothing at 10 P.M.).

Indiana:

10/3 (15 seconds) — Description of Bayh's call for Justice Department review of *Indianapolis Star* indictments, over slide (shown at 6, cut to 10 seconds for 10 P.M.).

10/4 (20 seconds) — Story on Bayh issue proposal, from wire (shown at 6, nothing at 10 P.M.).

(No coverage Saturday, 10/5.)

10/6 — Mention of Bayh in story reporting Lugar charge that Bayh sold a vote to the maritime union; (15 seconds) — story of Bayh calling for dismissal of Ford economic aides, both stories from wire (shown at 6 and 10 P.M.).

10/7 — Mention of Bayh in story on women's meeting, showing silent film of woman talking on Bayh's behalf; (75 seconds) story of Democratic county chairman posing questions he thought Lugar should be asked, no mention of Bayh (shown at 6 P.M.).

(No coverage Tuesday, 10/8.)

10/9 (15 seconds) — Tell story quoting Bayh opposing surtax (along with 15 seconds of Lugar saying the same thing), from wire (shown at 6 P.M.).

(No coverage Thursday and Friday, 10/10 and 10/11.)

10/12 (3 minutes, 50 seconds) — Story on the Senate campaign, including 1 minute, 40 seconds on Bayh. Bayh footage from a press conference that morning. Reporter quoted Bayh as opposing the surtax (opening statement at press conference) and used film of Bayh answering a question saying the race looked good, but it would depend on turnout (the theme of the piece was that Lugar was in trouble due to surtax and his campaign manager) (shown at 5 and 10 P.M.).

Massachusetts:

10/14 (20 seconds) — Sargent comments on Rockefeller's confirmation in light of Goldberg book.

10/15 (1 minute, 40 seconds) — Sargent calls out National Guard to deal with busing crisis.

10/16 (20 seconds) — Anchorman reads story of Sargent and White (mayor of Boston) quarreling about decision to call out the guard.

10/16 (1 minute) — State GOP chairman says all incumbents should quit after one term, including Sargent, his party's incumbent candidate.

10/17 (1 minute) — Anchorman reads lead-in explaining that Dukakis and Sargent have refused the station's offer of debate time, then shows film of Dukakis explaining why.

10/18 (1 minute, 45 seconds) — Sargent's media event. Press conference accusing Dukakis of misleading public about tax hikes during Sargent years (25 seconds anchorman, 55 seconds Sargent on sound film, 25 seconds Dukakis' campaign manager rebutting).

10/20 (1 minute, 5 seconds) — Sargent answering two questions at television debate on another station, followed by 1 minute, 5 seconds of the political commentator bemoaning the boring format and forecasting defeat for Sargent unless a new issue arose.

10/21 (1 minute, 40 seconds) — Sargent's claims on taxes labeled "lies" by Democratic state legislators. Anchorman reads Sargent's spokesman's denial. More commentary.

10/22 (50 seconds) — Lieutenant governor and Dukakis on film talking about taxes. They disagree. Reporter adds a report from an independent tax group suggesting both are lying.

10/23 (50 seconds) — Anchorman reads wire story on that night's televised debate, a story about Sargent's lawyer's defense of allegedly illegal campaign loan, and a third story of Dukakis on subject of Sargent loan.

10/23 (2 minutes) — Equal coverage of debate and commentary including state GOP chairman. Discussion of controversial Sargent ad on taxes. Conclusion: it's confusing but politics is always confusing.

10/24 (1:30) — More commentary: this format of debate was more exciting. Do it again.

On analysis, the log reveals five areas of television coverage:

- general themes of the campaign, such as the economy and experience in office.

- specific but minor issues, usually the subject of a planned visual;

- comments on current events that were elicited by the press rather than dramatized by the campaign, such as Sargent commenting on Rockefeller's appointment;

- statements about the campaign's prospects (often referring to poll data); and

- charges and attacks on the opposition.

The more personal, less issue-oriented areas appear to have been initiated by the press rather than by the campaign. Even so, one impact of television has been to make campaigns *more* issue-conscious than they were before the rise of the electronic media. For one thing, those old-style political rallies were staged events where one candidate would get up, recite the campaign slogans, and tell the assembled faithful what good fellows all the other candidates on the ticket were and how they were all going to march to victory on election day. Cynicism, deceit, and artificiality notwithstanding, a campaign has to suggest that something of importance is going to take place in order to get the assignment editor of a television station to send a crew out to cover a story. Television time, after all, is money, and the limited resources the stations devote to political coverage in terms of staff assignments heighten the competition among campaign organizations.

As campaign organizations compete for media time with each other and with all the fascinating news of the day — fires, plane crashes, and international developments — the focus of competition is confrontation. Confrontation with issues is presented by the campaign visual, which has the advantage of being dependent only on the imagination of the campaign staff and no one else. Confrontation with the opposition is fostered by the media more often than by the campaign, because media staff can ask a candidate what he or she thinks of the opponent. Television news producers prefer visual stories over what are called "talking heads," that is, interviews of a candidate attacking the opponent. It is in the desire to show confrontation that the impact of television has lessened the likelihood of dialogue on issues. It must not be forgotten, however, that the dialogue we speak of so longingly has rarely been realized in American politics, and when it has, it was often in the context of a dramatic shift of political alignments.

Edward Jay Epstein notes that because of the Fairness Doctrine stations try to balance coverage. A story about one candidate will be matched to a story about the opposition, usually on the same subject. Balance, according to Epstein, is to be differentiated from truth because "the correspondent, after reporting the news happening, juxtaposes a contrasting viewpoint and concludes his synthesis by suggesting that truth lies somewhere in between."[3] This is precisely the way the Massachusetts tax story was covered. The lieutenant governor, the Democratic candidate, and a third independent tax group were all given air time. It would be unusual indeed to see a television reporter covering two candidates and concluding by saying that Candidate X told the truth and Candidate Y was lying through his teeth.

Television is bound by its technology. It must necessarily offer a *different* kind of campaign coverage than a newspaper, which depends only on its reporters' access to the candidate or other knowledgeable sources. Newspaper reporters usually report anything new or unusual a candidate says during the day, even if he says it to only a few reporters. Television stations can read their audiences a condensation of what the newspapers have reported, but they much prefer to show the

---

[3]Edward Jay Epstein, *News from Nowhere: Television and the News* (New York: Random House, 1973), 67.

candidate in action, if such film can easily and cheaply be obtained. That is, they prefer an interview with the candidate answering questions in a press conference, especially if a question is put by their reporter. That suggests as much about the reporter and station as it does about the candidate. Newspapers can print several paragraphs about the candidate's remarks, allowing the attentive reader to discern the context and nuances; television stations must present the barest possible summary of the candidate's opinion. By virtue of their space flexibility, lower cost of coverage, and the absence of the Fairness Doctrine or right-to-reply rules, newspapers are freer to develop "background" stories by interviewing "informed sources" (friends, campaign aides, enemies). The worth of such stories depends on the wisdom and fairness of the reporter, but they are always more extensive than what television can afford to produce. By looking in detail at how newspapers and television stations are organized, these differences can be more easily understood.

Organizational Differences

Newspaper news is gathered by a highly decentralized organization. Typically, a city room is a large open space with a number of desks squeezed in for the reporters and a separate area — a raised platform or a glassed-in cubicle — for the editors. Decisions about what to cover are usually made by the reporter and editor together, though often a reporter makes a decision alone, relying more on good sources and the concerns of fellow reporters on other newspapers. Because reality is difficult to discern in politics under the best of circumstances, political reporters may be even more dependent on what Paul Weaver described as his "specialist work group" — that is, other political journalists. This environment of uncertainty is akin to that which besets the campaign organization.[4]

---

[4]Paul Weaver, "The Metropolitan Newspaper as a Political Institution: An Organizational Analysis of the New York Press" (unpublished Ph.D. dissertation, Harvard University, September 1967), 227.

Decentralization places more responsibility on and gives more freedom to a newspaper reporter than a television reporter. Reporters carry around in their heads a rather complete image of the journalist as craftsman. Since newspaper reporters go through a fairly established apprenticeship system (from copyboy on up to having one's own by-line), that image is perpetuated from one generation to the next. Because newspapers rarely fire reporters there are usually several generations working together in the same newsroom, which helps maintain the tradition.

Individuality and self-reliance are among the most important values of the reporter's craft. Both values are maintained by nonparticipation. The reporter is an observer — adamantly so — of the events he or she covers. The decentralized nature of newspapers and reporters' lack of participation in political organizations free them from many of the constraints that organizations normally impose upon their members. That freedom from constraint, however, also results in an absence of cooperative experience. Whereas campaign organizations are composed of people who are constantly seeking the same things (money and the candidate's time) and must compromise with each other, reporters have no such need. Whereas the pressures in campaigns are such that decisions are often made informally by whoever is available, regardless of their positions in the organizational hierarchy, a reporter reaches a decision either alone or by appealing to others higher up. The job of a reporter is to write the truth, and truth depends on objectivity. Nonparticipation helps assure objectivity; so does an attitude of looking for reality beneath the surface. According to Weaver, scepticism "is one of the principal tools for apprehending reality. . . . As copyboys and cubs, all reporters learn not just to doubt, but to doubt constantly, constitutionally, almost passionately. . . ."[5]

Television is a different world entirely. It is not that the television reporter is less interested in truth (though he or she is more interested in balance), but rather that success is measured differently. On a newspaper, a reporter succeeds by the

---

[5]*Ibid.*

ability to uncover a story and write it quickly and accurately; a television station measures the quality of the reporter's delivery. Rating systems are refined enough to provide information on the size and nature of an audience and on its attitudes toward different media personalities.

Because television measures are so exact and are beyond the ability of any individual to control, they tend to encourage a more bureaucratic organizational structure. That tendency is reinforced by the limits of technology and time, which combine to reduce much decision making to routine procedure. The routinization extends even to decisions about what news will be covered, which comes under the heading of "expected" news — that is, news events which provide sufficient warning before they occur to enable the station to dispatch a film crew to the scene. Campaign visuals fit nicely into that category.

The most important factor in television's decision making about what news to cover is what news will be visually interesting and entertaining. As television stations increasingly depend on news programming to provide revenue, instead of the public service required for licensing by the FCC, local news formats have had less time for political reporting. As local outlets turn more and more to outside consultants to increase the revenues generated by news shows, the shows have grown similar in format. We have gone, in recent years, from news shows where reporters read their copy much as they would have written it for newspapers to "happy talk" shows on which there is considerable by-play between members of the on-camera news staff and where the stories selected each evening are chosen for their viewer appeal. This change reflects the realization that local news shows, far from merely discharging a public responsibility, can be entertainment vehicles and as such can make money. How any given story is written for a newspaper, even an entire edition, does not affect revenues significantly.

The more routinized things get, the less room there is for individual expression, and the less likelihood of risk taking on the part of organization members. Among the television reporters interviewed in the study, there was a marked sense that they were just doing their jobs and trying to keep out of trouble. The exceptions to this rule stood out all the more because they were so unusual. The image of self-reliance and independence inculcated in newspaper journalists as they work their way up in their profession is absent among television reporters.

One reason they are not self-reliant is that they are dependent on the news makers to provide those expected filmable events. This greater dependence is indirectly related to program ratings. Reporters with low ratings do not have their contracts renewed. They move on, often to another state. There is considerable mobility in the television field, in contrast to newspapers, and the consequences of mobility are particularly hard on political reporters, who rely more heavily on cultivating sources than do other kinds of journalists.

For all the differences between a newspaper and a television station, there are differences still greater between their two kinds of organizational environments and that of a campaign. Neither the individualistic world of a newspaper reporter nor the bureaucratic world of a television reporter prepares their members to understand the workings of such an ad hoc organization. There is a tendency to impute rationality where it is not and to miss it where it does occur. To the reporter who goes back and forth between campaigns during an election, the campaign organizations appear to be focused entirely on the opposition. To an insider, most of the conflict is within the campaign organization, and there is relatively little attention paid to the opposition. Because reporters ask rational questions they get rational answers, and it is not surprising that there are marked differences in perceptions of reality between members of a campaign organization and members of the press. Without exception, each member of a campaign who had previously been a member of the press said he or she would have been a better reporter had he had some experience on the inside of a political organization.

The press coverage of the McGovern campaign in 1972 was heavily descriptive of the tensions that beset the organization. Media descriptions of the Nixon campaign gave the impression of a well-oiled machine, an impression that changed only with the televising of the Watergate hearings, which opened a window for the public on what was actually going on inside the organization. The Democratic campaign, by contrast, was unusually open. The press, never having seen so much of a campaign organization before, was impressed by the disorder. Having nothing to compare it to either in their own experience or in relation to other presidential campaigns, they concluded it was unusually chaotic — a conclusion that may well have affected a portion of the vote in November. Yet there is considerable evidence to suggest that the McGovern campaign was not more disorganized than any other campaign.[6]

There are, of course, other reasons for differences in the perceptions of members of the press and politicians. The most important is their difference in objectives. The campaign wants to tell a story that will attract support, which it does by presenting a rational, planned public face; and the press wants to tell the "truth," which means, as often as not, presenting the unplanned and the irrational happenings in a campaign. One side is pleased if a story comes out the way they planned it, the other if it comes out in a way that was clearly unplanned.

Campaign Responses to the Media

There is no question that television can generate an air of excitement. That is one of the appeals of politics for those who like being in the center of things. In presidential campaigns, where network news programming is the only national medium available, television is critically important in keeping the campaign alive in the electorate's mind as the candidate travels back and forth across the country. Statewide campaigns try to use television the same way, but it is a less efficient medium for reaching voters at the state level than the one or two large newspapers in each state. Nonetheless, campaigns allocate a considerable portion of their primary resource — the candidate's time — to doing visuals and being available to the electronic media.

---

[6]Xandra Kayden, "The Political Campaign as an Organization," *Public Policy*, vol. 21 (Spring 1973), no. 2.

There are three reasons for this focus on television. (1) Television news does reach a lot of people, and what appears on it is perceived to be important just because it appears. (2) Presidential campaigns concentrate on television, and politicians at all levels tend to imitate presidential techniques of gaining media attention. (3) Planning visuals for television provides for a complementary relationship between the two organizations, making it easy for one to meet the needs of the other.

In order to understand the impact of television coverage of campaigns, it is appropriate to consider what they were like before television. This is not easily done because along with the advent of television has come a change in the political process itself. In the halcyon days of yore, before electronic media, politics was, as much as anything else, a form of entertainment. It was the time when ward politics was alive and machines dominated American cities and many counties. Tradition has it that torchlight parades and large rallies of the faithful were commonplace events in the political season from Labor Day to election day. There was a certain kind of enjoyable camaraderie to be gained from participating in these old-time political meetings. But with the advent of television particularly (and also the reformers of the 1950's) rallies were less often seen, partly because more people could be reached with television and partly because reformers could not easily produce big rallies. It is also true that people are becoming afraid to go out at night.

Television has made us feel more sophisticated about this style of politics. It has shown us the mechanical underpinnings of such events. When it filmed scenes of supporters waiting in the wings for their cues it took away much of their impact by revealing their unspontaneous nature. With its penchant for filming the unplanned, television made the traditional events seem artificial. Campaign managers grew wary that something might go wrong. The candidate might be heckled or the turnout might be small. Scenes would turn up on the evening news that damaged the candidacy just because they were unplanned happenings.

Television is an intimate medium. Rallies were large events, planned to encourage the faithful. The visual is often a confrontation between a candidate and an issue, usually provided by a concerned citizen who helps dramatize the issue at hand in a way suitable for home viewing. For the home viewer, the visual personalizes the issue and the candidate along with it. Other kinds of confrontations might take place, which may or may not include other people, but an essential to the campaign visual is the setting in which events take place. They must be in places that are familiar and filmable. Candidates visiting a playground talk about education; at a gas station, they are concerned with energy and the rising cost of fuel. It is difficult to film a candidate talking to a machinist at a factory or a hospital patient in bed, because cameras and television lights are still rather cumbersome gadgets.

The campaign visual is thus issue-oriented. It must be so in order to entice the television assignment editor to send out a film crew to cover it. Because the issues are often peripheral to the campaign, a visual can be described as a dramatization of current events, enabling the candidate to make clear to the voters where he or she stands on the issues in the headlines of that day or week. The issues tend to be peripheral because there is usually a limit to the number of imaginative ideas the campaign staff can come up with to dramatize the major issues. The visuals that were covered during the study included such topics as mental health, strip mining, and prison reform.

Although visuals are part of the daily campaign schedule, each time the campaign has something important to say it calls a press conference and makes no attempt to use props or a setting in order to get the message across. Such was the case, for example, in Tennessee when Lamar Alexander responded to a charge made by his opponent that he was not talking about issues, and he (the Democratic nominee) would not debate Alexander until he did. Both the charge and the countercharge were made in press conferences.

Why, we often inquire, do not candidates stand for principles? Why do not campaigns offer a choice of positive alternatives from which the voter can make a rational choice? The press is part of the problem. The fact that press conferences are taken more seriously by both the press and the campaign points up an interesting aspect of political coverage. Much of what is perceived to be news comes under the heading of charge and countercharge. The press fosters that style. Aside from the debate about the role of the press in reporting political events, there is a long-standing antipolitical tradition in this country, which leads most Americans to accept a politician's word on things with a grain of salt. A number of the stories monitored during the study were press initiated: the press would goad one candidate to react to charges made by the opponent. Examples of this included a response by Alexander to Blanton's visual on prison reform, another response by Alexander to a poll by Blanton showing the Democrat substantially in the lead, Dukakis attacking Sargent's handling of a loan, and Sargent accusing Dukakis of misleading the public about tax hikes. Because television seeks balance, its coverage does not permit the development of a theme or a platform on which a candidate can offer himself or herself to the voter. Balance has come to mean instead charge and countercharge, with an assumption that truth lies somewhere in between. Television encourages interplay between candidates in such a way as to lead to the assumption that both are lying.

Even though the press (particularly television) encourages confrontation, it still plays a valuable role in focusing on issues, particularly when it exercises its independence and does investigative reporting. Some circumstances are more conducive than others for investigative reporting. Local tradition is one factor. Another appears to be the presence or absence of a press corps. Timothy Crouse in *The Boys on the Bus* made the interesting point that if campaign reporters travel in a group and have no social contacts outside that group and the candidate's press office — as is the case in a presidential campaign — the reporters will behave like a pack following the leader. If one says the crowd is enthusiastic at a campaign stop, everyone filing a story will describe the enthusiastic crowd.[7] In a statewide campaign the press corps do not travel. They exist in a relatively stable environment in which many sources of information are available. They are neither isolated, as their

---

[7]Timothy Crouse, *The Boys on the Bus* (New York: Random House, 1972).

counterparts in a presidential race are, nor as totally dependent on the campaign staff for information.

Of the campaigns studied, the only one with a press corps in attendance was in Massachusetts. There is a press corps in Indianapolis, but it concentrates on city hall or the statehouse, not on a campaign for the Senate. *The Indianapolis Star,* in fact, won a Pulitzer Prize in 1974 for its investigative reporting of a scandal in the local police department. It was able to follow through on stories about Lugar's administration as the city's mayor, but it was not in a position — nor did it really try — to do any serious investigative writing about Birch Bayh's record in the Senate. In Tennessee, there was a gubernatorial race in the state capital, but because neither candidate was an incumbent their organizations were relatively unknown to the local press.

Press corps appear when the activity is large enough in scope to provide news on a daily basis. It takes a lot of people to create that much activity, thereby providing the press with multiple opportunities for information. And because there are a number of reporters, there is also some measure of competition for stories. For the campaign, having a press corps means not only getting the media to cover a given event, but also being able to respond to information gathered independently by the press. This situation was illustrated in Massachusetts when a few young reporters uncovered what appeared to be an illegal loan from Sargent's wife to his campaign. As Tom Reardon, Sargent's press secretary, noted afterwards, "On the loan thing, you don't know what's happening yourself, and you are reluctant to learn simultaneously with reporters what's happening. You want to know what the total story is going to be. When the report came in, no one knew what the real story was on the loan. We at least had the advantage of knowing it was not done out of malice, and we were fairly open, but you are always aware that things can happen and headlines at the end of a campaign can have a devastating effect. It is open, but there is always the danger of misinterpretation."

The loan story had come to the attention of the Sargent people late one afternoon two weeks before the election. Several reporters were looking at the finance records filed by the campaign with the state in compliance with a new law. A few days earlier, this same group of reporters had uncovered violations of the law by one of the candidates for secretary of state — the candidate, it happened, who had written the law while a member of the state legislature. The reporters approached Jack Flannery, Sargent's chief secretary, who said he knew nothing about the loan and suspected it was a technical error. He began making phone calls to find someone who did know what had happened and who could answer the reporters' questions. Flannery pointedly refused to let the reporters speak to the governor, even though at least one of the phone calls made in their presence was to Sargent. Knowing that Sargent knew nothing about the issue, Flannery wanted to prevent any headlines quoting the governor that might prove embarrassing. He cautioned the reporters against asking questions of people who said they knew nothing about the issue.

Although the reporters agreed with Flannery that the loan report was probably a technical error, they disagreed with him as to whether or not it was appropriate for them to write about it. From their perspective, the record was clear — an illegal loan had been recorded, and whether or not the record was in error, it was a story. "How can you write a story if you don't know the answer to the major question?" they were asked by Bob Caulfield, a member of the governor's staff who had considerable experience in the media himself. "It's reported," responded one of the reporters. "We can't wait on the story, because there is a competitive side to this business and someone else could beat us to it." The deadline for the first edition of the newspaper was 9:30, and the reporters agreed to wait in their office at the statehouse for a phone call from the governor's chief counsel, who would give them all the information he could gather.

The story took several days to play itself out in the press. Some media organizations took it more seriously than others. The assignment editor for one local television station decided not to cover it because it was, after all, only a question of a candidate's borrowing money from his wife, which did not seem too egregious an error. The statehouse staff spent many hours over the next week trying to understand what actually happened, and how to persuade the press to end the story as soon as possible. Paul Guzzi, the candidate for secretary of state, wanted to hold a joint press conference with Sargent, but the governor's staff decided against it, wanting to avoid having the governor say anything (beyond the ambiguous statements he had made the morning after the meeting in Flannery's office, when he was approached directly by reporters). As Flannery noted, "If we join in the press conference with Guzzi it's a Sargent headline. If we are just part of the Guzzi story, we would be in the seventh paragraph."

It is interesting to note that for several days the story was an issue between the campaign staff and the press. The fight gained momentum when it was turned into a campaign issue by other political actors: the Republican State Committee chairman — not an ally of Sargent's — who said that if Sargent were guilty he should resign from the ticket; and the Democratic gubernatorial candidate, Michael Dukakis, who said that Sargent was trying to invoke a Watergate coverup. At that point, the issue began to turn in Sargent's favor. Dukakis had overreacted, and the sensibility of the television assignment editor who initially chose to ignore the story began to prevail: it was possibly an illegal loan from the candidate's wife, certainly not an abuse of power or a coverup, as the Watergate allusion suggested. Sargent began to use it to advantage by playing up the humor of the situation, suggesting it was not a good thing to borrow from one's wife — especially at the commercial rate of 12 percent.

The Sargent loan issue points out a number of interesting elements in the relationship between the campaign and the press. The story had greater credibility coming from the reporters than it did coming from the opposition. When, in fact, political enemies began to get into it, they lessened the impact of the issue and helped make Sargent look like a hapless underdog. The campaign staff wanted the issue to go away, and to avoid any statements that might lead to an embarrassing headline late in the campaign when they might not have time to turn the story to their advantage. Embarrassment could come from any quarter within the organization, from the candidate on down, and Flannery tried to direct access by the press, to limit that possibility. The reporters accepted Flannery's direction, relying on what appeared to be a long-standing relationship between them. The investigative tendencies of the reporters notwithstanding, if the Sargent campaign staff had in fact been trying to hide something about the loan from the press, they probably would have succeeded, because the reporters were dependent on the continuing relationship for their news sources and did not want to push Flannery too hard. It was not totally fortuitous that the Watergate scandal was uncovered by reporters working for a city desk, not by the White House press corps. Woodward and Bernstein had no on-going relationships to jeopardize. A political environment large enough to provide news for a press corps is an important ingredient in investigative reporting. Having a press corps, however, is not in itself an assurance that there will be investigative reporting. It encourages competition, which is positive, but it depends on continuing relationships that require restraint.

The Media and Democratic Theory

Politicians are like actors in search of a play. People run for public office because they want to be in public life. The issues they run on are, as often as not, a justification for candidacy, not a cause of it. E. E. Schattschneider and V. O. Key have posed questions about the consequences of how the electorate is offered a choice, and how the dialogue of most campaigns excludes relevant questions for segments of the electorate.[8] But if one looks to the media as a cause of such neglect or unresponsiveness, one must also look at the nature of campaign coverage. Of the five areas of media coverage (major themes, minor issues, comments on current events, campaign prospects, and charges and countercharges), only one is probably irrelevant for making a choice (statements about the campaign's prospects). That one, however, is an important element in

---

[8]E. E. Schattschneider, *The Semi-Sovereign People* (New York: Holt, Rinehart and Winston, 1960); V. O. Key, Jr., *The Responsible Electorate* (Cambridge: Harvard University Press, 1966).

maintaining a campaign organization by building morale and encouraging fund raising.

The visuals on minor issues personalize them in a way that is probably educational, if not critical, and they can be of interest to particular groups. Comments on current events are valuable for understanding a candidate's attitudes on a spectrum of issues, an important consideration for choosing someone for public office. Charges and countercharges can clarify a candidate's position on things, perhaps more then he or she might have wished. They can also obfuscate to the point where it is difficult to tell who said what to whom or why, particularly when public attention is rather casual.

Without the media the average voter would know the candidate's party label and perhaps might have heard the candidate speak. (Labels are still the most important factor in how people cast their ballots.) But the traditional campaign speech is no help to a voter faced with making a choice. It consists of statements on the major themes of the campaign and the importance of the candidate's election, such as Bayh's recitation of what he did for Indiana, or Sargent explaining why he could promise not to raise taxes. The speech may be valuable to hear, but it usually gets little media attention. The reporters have heard it too often; to them it is no longers "news." The need to keep the press interested is the reason campaigns produce visuals and press releases on a daily basis on such a wide variety of minor topics.

If the relationship between the media and the campaign fosters a proliferation of issues, from whence comes the charge that the media has lessened the substantive content of campaigns? One must consider who makes it. Political scientists and political journalists are probably the largest group. It may be, however, that their standards are inappropriate. Academics have a tendency to overvalue the role of ideas and research. Unless campaigns publish position papers on a wide spectrum of issues, they may not meet scholarly standards. The best political journalists read seriously the work of political scientists. They may be unduly influenced themselves, and of course they pay very close attention to the campaigns, far more than anyone else, probably far more than the people in one campaign organization pay to their opposition.

Elections are the process by which democratic societies function. The substantive content — particularly what candidates promise to do once elected — is no more significant than the process to which the candidates submit themselves. Most elections are mechanisms of accountability: People vote their approval or disapproval of the behavior of the previous administration. This is not an unreasonable voting determinant, particularly when one considers the complexity of most issues and the difficulty of keeping campaign promises where conditions change and branches of government check one another. Michael Dukakis offered a "leadpipe guarantee" that he would not raise taxes if he were elected governor of Massachusetts. He was elected and he has raised taxes. Would it not have been more important to know that the candidates understood how the offices they sought functioned, and how they functioned under stress in resolving the very real conflicts which government must resolve?

I would hardly argue against forcing candidates to take positions on issues. It is important for voters to know with whom they tend to agree. But positions can change with the circumstances, and what is obvious one day may be a little more complex the next. Campaigns are as much process as substance. If one looks at the energy a campaign organization devotes to organizational maintenance compared to what it expends on issue research, it is clear that, from the campaign perspective, process far outweighs substance. That process is another method of conveying information to the voters. With the increased communication about issues the media provide, today's voters know far more than their predecessors. If they wanted to know even more, it is quite likely the campaign would supply it. If nothing else, campaigns adapt to reality, at least as far as they are able to perceive it.

Chapter 7

The Campaign and the Electoral Process

This study highlights the process by which decisions are made in campaigns. It is a personal, intense, and informal process. In many respects it is no different than the decision making that accompanies the political processes in all organizations, but there is one major difference in campaigns: they are temporary organizations. In order to understand them, therefore, one must understand the tasks they perform, the environment in which they exist, and the effect of the short time frame on the people who work in them.

One obvious consequence of the temporary nature of campaigns is the lack of feedback the organization receives on its activities. There are few opportunities to see the result of one's work and, therefore, few opportunities to correct mistakes. The lack of feedback compounds the uncertainty that exists in all political environments. The uncertainty, in turn, forces organization members to look inward to their own strengths and weaknesses, and by looking inward to become relatively isolated from external circumstances and events. The reader may have noticed that there was very little mention of the opposing candidates in the preceding chapters, and certainly very little notice of the political climate of 1974.

Another consequence of the temporary nature of campaign organizations is that there are few constraints imposed on organization members. Because the job someone holds in a campaign is not permanent, there is little likelihood of an individual's developing strong internal links between himself and the job: his sense of identity will not be affected; he will not be known to his family and friends, or even to prospective employers, by the position held in a campaign. One effect of this lack of strong personal identity is that, however intense the campaign experience may be at the time, it does not have a long-term impact on campaign members. It is not unlike going to summer camp, the memories of which have faded by the time snow begins falling.

Another consequence of the lack of strong personal identity is that an individual will do whatever is required to get the job done — the "job" being the distribution of X number of bumper stickers or pieces of literature, not necessarily delivering X number of votes. Literature can be counted and measured; votes are much more difficult to be certain about, particularly before the main event. An election happens once. There is no second place and no second chance. The closer election day gets, the less means matter over ends and the fewer the constraints imposed on the completion of tasks.

Because the organization is temporary, there is relatively little time to socialize members into a uniform set of goals and pattern of behavior. For the vocationalists, the intensity of the campaign will overcome the short time frame; they will crowd more hours of the day and more days of the week into the campaign at the expense of other activities and of exposure to values held by people outside the organization. But the avocationalists, who are peripheral to the campaign, will not be deflected from their initial motivation or perception of what politics is all about. Since much of the activity of campaigns is of a routine nature and is carried out by the avocationalists, their work will be almost as consequential as the work of the full-time vocationalists. The values they hold when they come into the campaign are the values upon which they act. They are not changed by the experience, by the differing values held by other avocationalists or the full-time vocationalists.

Whether or not the vocationalists change is more questionable, but I think not. The commitment they make in time, energy, and single-minded devotion is made just because it is a temporary commitment. A too rigid personality might have problems coping with the stresses of organizational life, which are magnified in a campaign, but those who are less rigid can normally forgo some of the supports usually available to handle stress (such as a private home life), at least for the short run.

There are, however, some consequences of the temporary organization for the political process, even though it does not affect the people who are part of it. Because campaigns are temporary, they must devote an extraordinary amount of time to the creation and maintenance of their organization. The standard operating procedures that facilitate the operation of permanent structures must be established anew with each campaign. The patterns of authority (such as they are) must be created. And the organization must generate a sense of community or uniqueness for its members and for campaign watchers, who measure a candidate's potential by the nature of the campaign organization.

One might question the efficiency of a system that requires people to devote half their energy to their own circumstances and only half their energy to making their cause known. Would the democracy be better served by more permanent organizations, such as parties, or even by the growing number of professional campaign consultant organizations, which would lessen the need for so strong an inner focus? Before rushing to a conclusion, it would be wise to consider the role campaign organizations as they presently exist play in the political process.

Why do people come to work in campaigns? Many of the organizers spoke of their desire to perform some kind of public service, particularly at their time of life when they had few responsibilities that would suffer from such a commitment. The seekers used the organization as a platform from to reconsider their options, which might include a mid-career change to public service. The apprentices were there to learn and discover their aptitude for political careers. For the vocationalists, then, it could be said that campaigns provided an opportunity to explore their potential. They made a commitment, but because it was temporary, it was a tentative commitment with opportunity for evaluation on both sides.

The avocationalists made less of a commitment in terms of the sacrifices of their daily life, but of the three groups in this category, only the materialists expected a direct political return on their investment. The believers felt that participation enabled them to fulfill their civic responsibilities. And the joiners looked to campaigns to fulfill their social needs — a factor in everyone's participation. If campaign organizations were more permanent, it is quite likely that neither the believers nor the joiners would find much of a role. And if campaigns were more permanent, the organizations could not afford the materialists; it would be too costly to provide rewards for every favor given.

Would the political process be better served without the participation of the avocationalists? Clearly, the rewards they gain are private. Still, it is the avocationalists who are what might be called the shock troops — the people out on the front lines who do most of the door-to-door canvassing, telephoning, and so on. If voters are to have any direct contact with a campaign — other than the opportunity to see the candidate in person — chances are it will be with one of the avocationalists. Professional campaign consulting organizations cannot reach voters this way. Parties could if they employed volunteers, but if they did (as they used to), there would be little difference between the regular party volunteers and the avocationalists in the campaign, with the possible exception that there might be a higher proportion of materialists in the group. We may, in fact, be coming to this with the implementation of the federal election law, which may give a boost to party structure because of the limits it imposes on campaigns. If we increase the role of the party in supplying volunteers, questions to consider are what it is that motivates people to volunteer, and whether their incentives are appropriate to the process.

On the whole, the campaign organization can be said to be a testing ground for people who are considering a public service career. Permanent government service may be less rigorous in terms of the time commitment, though this is not necessarily the case. It will bear many resemblances to the campaign organization, particularly in the nature of decision making, which must always be carried out in a complex and uncertain environment.

It should also be noted that elections bring more people into office than those whose names are on the ballot. All elected officials are to some degree or another dependent on their staffs, and those elected to executive office have an even greater need to measure the worth of those they will appoint, whether to staff or line positions. Insofar as campaigns are testing grounds, they serve the political process well.

On the other hand, is that not a rather expensive way to go about testing the value of potential public servants? And are there not other costs to the political process because of the inward focus of campaign organizations? Each of the organizations studied could be said to have constructed an elaborate game, with rules, rewards, and penalties, that it played out for several months until election day. The game board was delineated not so much by the political boundaries of a state as it was by the limits of the organization itself. It did not include the opposition, and for the most part, it did not include the political environment of America in the fall of 1974. The issues each campaign attempted to raise were not totally irrelevant to that environment, but they were self-contained. They were designed to show the candidate off to best advantage, and wherever possible to show up the weaknesses of the opposition. But the issues, whether appropriate or not, were not that germane to the campaign organization as a whole. What was germane was the distribution of literature (albeit issue-oriented literature), the number of people brought to a fund raiser or a meeting, getting a letter to the editor published, and getting a visual broadcast on the six o'clock news. Any or all of these objectives *could* lead to a vote, *could* elucidate the candidate's position on an issue or draw a distinction between the candidate and his opponent, but the only measurement is that the task gets done. Perhaps some day we will solve the problem of using air time in an equitable way, and television will indeed supplant the traditional tasks that campaigns perform. Or perhaps some day we will come to the conclusion that these tasks can be performed in other ways or replaced by tasks that will enable the campaign to measure their impact on voters. Certainly we should consider alternatives.

Campaign practices have been given considerable attention in the last few years because of the Watergate scandal, although campaign reform was under way before 1972, and reform itself happens almost cyclically in our history. Nevertheless, the unveiling of the activities of the Committee to Re-Elect the President and the White House opened the eyes of many Americans to how the process works, or at least to how it worked in the Nixon Administration in 1972. Moral questions were raised concerning issues of influence and fair play (the dirty tricks) in campaigns, which may or may not obscure a free election.

Influence in campaigns comes down to two questions: Do people contribute to campaigns because they expect a return on their investment in the form of favorable legislation or favorable treatment from an officeholder? And do politicians solicit donations with the intention of looking after those who contribute and making enemies of those who do not? The answer to both questions is to be found in the attitudes of the participants. The believers, who give of their time and their money to fulfill their civic responsibilities, expect no return. The materialists, on the other hand, believe they should receive a return on their investment, but their beliefs may not necessarily correspond with those from whom they would seek favor. In other words, the givers may believe they are giving because it is necessary to grease the wheels of government, but the candidate, and especially the candidate's staff, may not agree.

It would be naive to suggest that influence is never offered nor sought, but it would be equally naive to assume that this is the norm in politics. There are situations which are more likely to be conducive to corruption, particularly at the local level, where the goods and services that are the rewards of office are concrete and clear, or at the state level where a single industry or interest dominates. And there are occasions when people who win office hold the same beliefs as the most pessimistic materialists. If one can accept at face value the statement made by most of the organizers that they were participating in politics because they derived pleasure from the opportunity to be in public service, and that they did not intend to spend the rest of their lives performing such service, it is not likely that they would be as vulnerable to influence-seekers as the materialists would expect.

As for the candidates, those who seek office will more and more be drawn from the ranks of the organizers. Two out of the six candidates for office in the three elections could already be said to be of that group: Lamar Alexander and Michael Dukakis. But even if the candidates were not drawn from this generation, there is still little reason to believe them motivated primarily by the desire to tabulate lists of their friends and enemies. Candidates seek office for a variety of reasons, not the least of which is the desire to wield influence. But the arena of the elected official's interest is different from the private contributor's. The official seeks influence with other officials over public issues; the private contributor seeks influence over public issues for private purposes. Whether the objective is collective or selective, the arena in which it must be sought is public, and the public actor (the politician) is the primary player. Politicians must work out the compromises required for the distribution of public goods and services, and they must work it out among themselves. There are interest groups, and there are always observers of the process (not the least of which is the press), but public actors must come to terms with each other. Hence they look to each other, seek to wield influence over each other, and maintain what might be called reciprocal relationships with each other. Private actors may have stronger private stakes in the game, but they are weaker in terms of their ability to exert influence.

Edward C. Banfield, in *Political Influence*, draws interesting distinctions among different kinds of influence and observes that to measure influence one must know not only what the influence seeker is able to achieve, but at what cost he achieves it.[1] The materialist can contribute to a campaign once, or even several times, over a series of campaigns, but there is usually a limit to what he can do for the politician and the politician for

---

[1]Edward C. Banfield, *Political Influence* (New York: The Free Press, 1961), 3–6.

him. There is, therefore, a limit to what he can ask of the politician, and with increased public disclosure of the relationships there is likely to be an even greater limit.

On the other hand, the politician, as a public servant, is very often eager to do favors for constituents (or potential constituents), even if they have not contributed to his election in the past, because there is always the hope they will contribute in the future. For a political figure, the next election is always the most important one. For all practical purposes then, a past contributor is in no better position than a noncontributor if there is a chance that the noncontributor will donate money for the next campaign. For whatever reasons, politicians organize their offices to handle requests; it is the central task of many of their assistants. There is, therefore, not quite a quid pro quo in politics. Political actors trade favors with other political actors, and although the private contributor has some stake in the action, he has only a secondary role.

This situation may be different in states dominated by a single industry, such as mining or automobile production, or states where one party is dominant, but domination by either a single industry or a single party appears to be a passing phenomenon. The more interest groups there are in a political community, the less likely it will be that the elected official or his staff will be dependent on any single figure or group of figures outside the public arena. This is, in fact, the reasoning of James Madison in the Tenth Federalist Paper and it seems to be substantiated by what I observed in this study.[2]

The diversity and complexity of the political community results in greater freedom for elected officials, enabling them to act according to the values they choose. Both incumbents in the study had "things to explain" to their constituents, particularly Sargent, who alienated much of his Republican constituency without replacing it with another, more liberal body of supporters for his programs. The uncertainty is so intense, however, that one is never sure what the constituents want in any case and

---

[2]*The Federalist Papers* (ed. Roy P. Fairfield), 2nd ed. (New York: Doubleday, 1966), 16–23.

therefore one's own judgment assumes greater importance.[3] The multiplicity of interest groups is another reason public figures are able to choose their priorities. A third reason is the fact that most political decisions are made with regard to other political figures in an environment relatively isolated from the voters. The question is, then, what are the values political actors bring with them into public life; how can they be assessed; and how can they be controlled?

Most theories of political participation and democracy suggest that complex democratic societies offer to and require of their citizens only the participation of voting. Citizens participate to the extent of choosing their rulers; more involvement would threaten social stability.[4] One of the most important values expressed by the activists of the 1960s was the value of participatory democracy. It was applied to other institutions as well as political ones, such as schools and universities. It is just this sense of inclusiveness and concern for the process that differentiates the current generation from previous political generations. It is different because it makes the exercise of power a group rather than an individual right. The group in question is limited to those who are a part of the political organization rather than the whole society, but if it does not change the society it does change the role of individuals who participate in politics. If it is true that each generation leaves an impact on the social structure, this will be the impact of the political organizers in the 1970s: a different sense of the exercise of power that plays down the role of the individual and is not dependent on charismatic appeal.

Assessing political actors depends on the communications media and the willingness of politicians to be assessed. Willingness in terms of campaigns can mean regularly scheduled debates, such as those held in Massachusetts, which enable voters

---

[3]A point corroborated by Warren E. Miller and Donald E. Stokes in "Constituency Influence in Congress," in Robert L. Peabody and Nelson W. Polsby, eds., New Perspectives on the House of Representatives (Chicago: Rand McNally, 1969), 51.

[4]For a discussion of this point see Carole Pateman, Participation and Democratic Theory (London: Cambridge University Press, 1970).

who watch them to get a measure of the men running for office. It is, of course, always a question whether that means one's positions on issues or one's humanity. Probably both.

Willingness can also mean an openness to the press, and that is a game at which two can play: the candidate's eagerness to gain positive visibility versus the reporter's desire to develop a good story — preferably one that is controversial. The objectives are both antithetical and parasitic. A look at the organizations involved also suggests that communications between members of the media and political actors are complicated by differences in experience with organizations: the ad hoc decision-making style of campaigning by whoever happens to be in the room at the time, the individualistic style of newspaper journalists, and the bureaucratic experience of television stations.

It is interesting to note that whenever one of the campaign organizations had something important to say, it called a press conference and did not bother with complicated techniques such as visuals to get the message across. The press conference is a format understood by all who participate in it; it is direct and to the point. Although there is a tendency for television news shows to run film only of their own reporter questioning the candidate, the intended message at least gets a hearing. The strength of the press conference is that it cuts through much of the uncertainty generated by organizational differences. It is as if it cut down on the organizational "noise." Another way to cut down on the "noise" would be to enable reporters (both print and electronic) to gain some experience inside political organizations. In support of this suggestion I would point to the statement made spontaneously by campaign members who had belonged to the press, that they would have been better reporters had they had such experience. Perhaps internships in campaigns should become part of the apprenticeship reporters go through in learning their craft.

One of the strongest conclusions that can be drawn from the organizational approach to the relationship between the media and the campaign is that the impact of the electronic media, particularly, has been to increase the flow of information to the voters. Television visuals were generated around issues and they had the effect of expanding the range of issues discussed in the campaigns. It is also true that without television, the debates scheduled in Massachusetts would not have had the impact they did, even though the most attentive audience were members of the press itself who translated their impressions to the voters.

The second issue of political morality that has been called into question lately and that may affect the outcome of an election is the role of dirty tricks in campaigning. Most of the tricks that have come to light are those designed to make a candidate look bad to the constituents and are in that sense public tricks. Some activities revealed by the Watergate hearings have been private: the break-in at the Democratic National Committee to gather information about donors to the party is a prime example. Of the two, it is undoubtedly the public tricks that are most threatening to the electoral process because they misrepresent the candidates and obscure the flow of information to the voters, which is so necessary for an intelligent choice. Clearly, some tricks are dirtier than others, and some are more damaging to the process than others. Heckling a candidate at a rally — thus forcing him to speak out on an issue he would rather avoid — adds to the flow of information. Misrepresenting someone's attitudes about segments of the population and becoming thereby an element in the person's decision to withdraw from the race — as was the case for Edmund Muskie during the New Hampshire primary — has a direct and important outcome on the choice voters are offered.

Temporary organizations do not affect the values of their members. If morality cannot be imposed in the development of standard operating procedures, then one must look to the values people bring with them into the organization. In campaigns, as in most political environments, having an impact on a decision requires conviction, enough imagination to come up with a plausible reason for that conviction, and the good fortune of being in the room when the decision is made. The important question to ask about the nature of political campaigning is who has access — who gets into the room.

The 1974 campaigns revealed a new generation of political actors in politics. The characteristics they share that differentiate them from their predecessors are largely stylistic in nature: they are organizationally oriented; they are working for the institutional process rather than against it; they are suspicious of charisma and power for its own sake; and they have a strong sense of personal efficacy. These characteristics are explainable in terms of their level of education, their place in the life cycle, and the time they came of age politically.

There is one important characteristic all politicians share, whether they be regular, amateur-reformer, or organizer: a preference for the process over the issues. Being a politician means being a part of the process. Issues are like chips that get moved around on a board, the means but not the ends of political life. The 1970s generation of political actors will not change the ideological component of American politics. It may change the institutions within the limits set by the temporary nature of campaigns.

But even if these changes do not measure up to the standards we would like to apply to campaigns, it may be that we need to make structural changes: we may need to change the time frame of campaigns — making them either shorter or longer. A shorter campaign might affect the expectations about how much of an organization to develop. If, for instance, a campaign were to last only two weeks, it is possible that campaign managers would not try to organize a field operation, and so on. Or we might make campaigns longer, which is to say permanent. If parties were responsible for campaigning, and were able to sustain an organizational structure from one election season to the next, it is conceivable they could develop the kinds of constraints we are seeking through the inevitable growth of standard operating procedures. Another element in the world of campaigns in recent years has been the growth of consulting firms. As permanent organizations, these companies will also have an impact on campaign behavior.

When we talk about campaign reform we mean more than financial constraints. For many reasons recent efforts at reform have been directed primarily at financing, but what is at issue is more than graft, it is the process itself. And it is the process which is probably least well understood, even, I would venture to say, by many who participate in it. Hopefully, an organizational analysis such as this would shed at least a small ray of light on the subject.

Chapter 8

Afterword: On Campaign Reform

I have suggested that understanding the nature of campaign organizations is extraordinarily important in understanding how campaigns function. But campaign organizations are temporary, ad hoc, and informal — in short, they are hard to regulate directly. If we are concerned about undue influence of large donors, or worried about the "dirty tricks" one campaign organization might play on another, it seems reasonable to try to regulate the primary — and one tangible — resource, that is, the funds. And it is in that direction that most campaign reform has been focused. Even if we cannot be sure of the impact money has on campaigns, we can at least measure it, and we can, therefore, regulate it. Whether such regulations will actually alter the way campaigns are conducted, of course, is another matter.

The campaigns studied in this book occurred in 1974. Two

years later, the first federal election was carried out under a new, extensive campaign reform law. Given what we know about campaign organizations, it seems appropriate to speculate on what the impact of campaign reform will be. Since the dynamics of campaign organizations do not change very much from one office to another, such speculation does not require a very great leap in imagination.

Campaign Reform in Perspective

The political system under which we now live is very much the product of reform brought about in response to past issues. Each political reform causes changes, sometimes expected, sometimes unexpected. And in some cases, correcting the mistakes of one reform effort leads to another reform effort.

Americans have spent much of this century weakening the political structures we feared were too strong. Parties have been the principal victims and, in the name of democracy, we have eliminated the parties as serious vehicles for accountability and change. We have also created a large, relatively permanent civil service, and we have attempted to limit and control the influence of special interest groups.

Until fairly recently, campaigns were not targets for reform efforts because until fairly recently, they were the creatures of parties. With the ever weakening control of parties over the nominating process, and with the rise of media as a tool for reaching the voters, campaigns have become separate organizational structures with only tenuous links to the parties under whose banner elections are presumably contested. The candidates who seek party endorsement are not selected by their peers. They are not screened for special qualifications or service to the party. Rather, they are a self-selected group of people whose most important asset is their capacity to put together enough of an organization to get on the ballot and run (at least in the primaries).

Since 1925, the principal control over campaign activities has been the Corrupt Practices Act. Although Congress made rather halfhearted attempts to pass updated versions of the law off and on in the intervening years, it was not until 1971 (a year before

Watergate) that an effective federal election campaign act came to be. It has been amended several times since, and altered by the Supreme Court as well, but it is now the major regulator of federal elections.

Campaign reform has been directed toward recording and controlling the money. If we know who gives and how much they give, we may have some indications of the kind of officeholder the candidate is likely to be. If we know how the money is spent, we may uncover undue attempts to influence voters. Another element in the focus on money has to do with conceptions of equality in a democratic society. There are varying degrees of acceptance of social and economic equality, but there is a view generally held (particularly by the Supreme Court in recent years) that political equality is a necessity. Hence one man, one vote. And hence the attempt to limit the influence of large donors, who might have undue influence in the political process.[1] It is also possible, however, that we focus on the money because it is measurable, and in the uncertain world of campaigns, measures are quite attractive.

On the one hand, one might argue that it does not matter what the specific nature of campaign reform is because campaigns will absorb changes, add whatever is necessary to comply to their repertoire, such as technical skills, and move on. Campaigns have already absorbed polling, paid media, visuals for getting on the evening news shows, and so on. On the other hand, the new laws and regulations may have a profound impact on campaigns and significantly alter the political process. This chapter will consider the possibilities of change in campaign organizations after analyzing the specific nature of the campaign reform legislation.

The Campaign Finance Law

The campaign law in effect in 1976 had the following broad objectives:

---

[1] David Adamany, "Money, Politics, and Democracy: A Review Essay," *The American Political Science Review*, vol. 71, no. 1 (March 1977), 289–304.

- limiting the influence of large donors;

- increasing participation of voters by inducing candidates to make broadly based appeals for support rather than relying on the donations of a few;

- minimizing or preventing deception or fraud on the part of the candidates and their workers in the course of an election;

- strengthening organized political parties; and

- ensuring the opportunity for people to run for office regardless of their personal wealth.[2]

The methods the law used to attain these objectives include the following:

- disclosure of campaign givers — what they have given and how it has been spent;

- limitations on campaign spending; and

- public financing of candidates.

In order to implement the law, Congress created the Federal Election Commission (FEC), which has regulatory responsibility over federal campaigns.

Disclosure

Much of the focus of the law has been on disclosure. Campaign organizations are required to submit periodic reports to the FEC detailing their income and expenditures. All contributions over $100 are disclosed, including the names, addresses, and occupations of the donors.

Reporting of contributions at the presidential level is necessary to obtain matching funds. Each contribution of $250 and

---

[2]The last two objectives were weakened by the Supreme Court in *Buckley v. Valeo* when it ruled, in the middle of the 1976 campaign period, that a limitation on spending of the candidate's personal wealth is a limitation of his First Amendment right of free speech. By weakening spending limitations, this thereby lessens the likelihood of parties' making independent expenditures on behalf of candidates. The impact of the nonlimitation of personal wealth by candidates will be to encourage rich candidates.

less can be matched by the federal government during the primary period.

Disclosing expenditures is like uncovering the skeletal structure of the campaign. Expenditures reveal the priorities of the campaign and the strategies it uses to play to its strengths and compensate for its weaknesses. Disclosure may also reveal illegal or inappropriate campaign activities, even though it can be argued that people intent on illegal activity can get around the procedure if they are inventive enough.[3]

Limitations

The second area of focus in campaign reform has been to limit the undue influence of large donors (both individuals and special interest groups). The limit any candidate for federal office may receive is $1,000 from an individual and $5,000 from a group. The limit an individual can give in any calendar year is $25,000. Since the average cost of a successful congressional campaign in 1976 was $86,000, and since the leading presidential candidates spent somewhere between $10 and $14 million during the 1976 primary period, it is clear that the influence of donors is significantly lessened at the presidential level and somewhat lessened at the congressional level.[4]

Another aspect of limitations concerns spending by the cam-

---

[3]A hypothetical example cited by an accountant in the 1976 presidential race to get around the $1,000 contribution limitation would be to ask the donor to give the campaign 25 $1,000 checks. The campaign would fill in 25 blank checks, gathered from around the country, with names and addresses taken from local telephone directories. The campaign would send one of the donor's checks to the bank each week and forward xerox copies of the false checks to the FEC at the same time. Unless the FEC asked the individuals whose names and addresses were used whether they in fact made a contribution (which could, presumably, be forestalled by obtaining permission), there would be no way for the commission to learn of the illegal contribution. Whether it is worth the time and effort to undertake such a fraud is another question.

[4]"A Study of the Impact of the Federal Election Campaign Act on the 1976 Election," prepared for the Federal Election Commission by Decision Making Information and Hart Research Associates (Washington, D.C., 1977), 2; and Kimball W. Brace, "The 1976 Presidential Primaries: An Analysis of How Many People Participated and How Much Money Was Spent," a report compiled for the Commission on Presidential Nomination and Party Structure, Democratic National Committee (Washington, D.C.), 4.

paign and independent supporters of the candidate. There are limits on how much a campaign can spend if it accepts public financing, and to a certain extent, on how the money can be spent. Ford was the only candidate of the 1976 presidential campaign to come close to reaching spending limits ($12 million in the primary and $21.8 in the general election). Since presidential campaigns are supported by public money as well as private donations, the limitations on expenditures make sense. The intent, however, was to equalize resources.

Public Financing

Public financing provides for matching grants during the primary period and total financing (thereby excluding private donations) during the general election. It currently applies only to presidential candidates. The obvious intent of the law is to force campaigns to appeal for support to many small donors instead of a few large donors.

In order to qualify for financing during the primaries, a candidate must raise $5,000 in each of 20 states from donations of $250 or less. A qualified candidate is eligible for up to $5 million in matching funds during the primary period, to be paid out against $250 contributions. In other words, if one donor gives a candidate $1,000 (the legal limit), only the first $250 can be matched, for a total of $1,250. On the other hand, if 100 donors give $250 contributions, each can be matched and they are worth $50,000 to the campaign. This assumes, of course, that each donation is properly reported to the Federal Election Commission. Needless to say, the accounting task becomes rather formidable. In the early years of the law, the legal questions were equally difficult to straighten out.

Public financing also extends to the two major parties. The Democrats and Republicans were each given $2 million for their national nominating conventions. Once the nominees were chosen, each accepted $21.8 million to run the campaign in the general election. As noted earlier, this foreclosed the option of accepting private donations. It was hoped that would-be donors during the general election would contribute up to $20,000 to the parties instead.

Although the reform law is principally directed toward campaigns, it originally intended to provide some support to the parties, particularly the two major parties. Minority parties and their candidates can qualify after the election for federal financing, but only after they can demonstrate that they received at least 5 percent of the vote. Efforts are being made to alter this to some extent, but a Congress organized around the two-party system is not likely to go far in seeking serious change that would favor third or minor parties.

Independent Expenditures

Since campaigns are limited as to the amount of money they can spend in elections (including the primary period), the law makes provision for supporters to express on their own their interest in a candidate. Corporations, labor organizations, trade associations, and so on may endorse candidates to their membership; groups may take out ads in newspapers to announce their support for a candidate; and groups and individuals may finance their own campaign literature.

Controlling independent expenditures is probably an impossible task since those charged with control would hardly know where to begin to look to find those involved. Furthermore, even to attempt such control could be a violation of the rights of free speech and the press. The law requires only that such expenditures be reported to the Federal Election Commission. It also requires that such expenditures be truly independent, which is to say that the initiation and the implementation of any project must be unrelated to the campaign.

The Federal Election Commission

Campaigns must file information about their contributors and their expenditures, and they can appeal to the FEC for formal or informal advice about activities or expenses they would like to incur. Consequently, the commission has become a "third partner" in the relationship between campaigns and the electorate. Although candidates for federal office have been filing reports for years with the General Accounting Office or their respective houses in Congress, the complexity of the law and the nature of the regulations have required most large campaign organizations to add accountants and lawyers to their staffs just to fulfill commission requirements.

As a regulator, however, the FEC is in a rather peculiar position. Its "partnership" in the process does not mean that it is dividing resources between competing interest groups. Voters are passive participants, especially during the course of the campaign. And the interests of one candidate in a race are not substantially different from the interests of another candidate in the race.

Most regulating agencies in the government seek compromise among the interests of several competing groups, and their success or failure is reflected in constituent responses to the members of Congress. For the FEC, however, congressmen are candidates as well as lawmakers, and they have a very direct interest in the decisions made by the FEC.

The problems of regulations are compounded when one thinks of the campaign organizations themselves. Because they are temporary, they have neither standard operating procedures nor personnel who can establish close working relationships with the commission staff (a situation alleviated somewhat at the presidential level, where candidates often establish headquarters in Washington, D.C.). Those intent upon subverting the law could probably get away with it, at least for a little while, but most campaigns have trouble understanding and complying with the regulations.

Speculations About the Impact of Reform on Campaigns

Assuming that the laws and regulations are equitably applied and that the complexity does not get out of hand, what is the potential impact of campaign reform on campaign organizations? If campaigns are flexible, given the uncertainty of their environment and the ebb and flow of pressures upon them, it is possible that the adjustment process will be fairly easy.[5] On the

[5]In support of this thesis was the attitude expressed by campaign finance people after the election. They were less concerned about the substance of the law and the regulations than they were about *knowing* what the law and regulations

other hand, it is also possible that these reforms will seriously affect the operations and dynamics of campaign organizations, and through them, the electoral process as a whole.

The following speculations fall into several categories: organizational changes, fund-raising changes, campaign-spending changes, and the relationship between campaigns and the rest of the political environment — the political parties and independent spenders.

Organizational Changes

Old-style fund raisers will be replaced by organizers. The strength of the old-style fund raisers lay in their ability to gain access to and money from a network of wealthy political patrons. Less and less will these people give of their time and energy to raise the small amounts of money prescribed by law. Finance departments in campaign organizations will come to resemble the rest of the organization in terms of the style, aspirations, and expectations of their members. The strength of the organizers will rest in their ability to put together political action committees and organize fund-raising events the way political organizers put together political events.

Accountants and lawyers will form a new department. Handling the administration of compliance with the campaign reform regulations requires professional expertise. It is possible that new departments will be added to campaign organizations. It is also possible that the accountants and lawyers who specialize in this area will work for several campaigns in the course of an election, and may maintain offices in a separate part of town or perhaps out of state altogether, like the people who produce paid media spots.

---

were. In other words, it does not matter what set of rules the game uses, as long as everyone has an equal chance of knowing what they are. See Xandra Kayden, "Report of a Conference on Campaign Finance Based on the Experience of the 1976 Presidential Campaigns," The Campaign Finance Study Group of the Institute of Politics, John F. Kennedy School of Government, Harvard University (Cambridge, 1977), 58–59.

Volunteer tasks at headquarters will change from envelope stuffing to record keeping. Volunteers may be used to make sure contributors provide all the information about themselves required by the FEC, and to code that information into a computer or transfer it to records to be submitted to Washington. Such a new use of volunteers in headquarters might prove pleasant and beneficial for both the volunteers and the campaign. It is the sort of labor-intensive task well suited to volunteers motivated by a solidary incentive.

Volunteer work in the field will decline. Compliance with the law has required campaigns to centralize decision making for both fund raising and spending. It is impossible otherwise to keep the necessary records. It is also possible that activities generated outside the central headquarters may exceed spending limits imposed by law, or by the central campaign itself. Either way the risk is one campaigns cannot afford. The quid pro quo traditionally expected by the materialists who participate in field organizations may be difficult to record, if not outright illegal. The most likely outcome will be a decline of local visibility for campaigns and an increase in centrally generated activity: fewer yard signs and more paid television.

Public financing may enable campaign organizations to plan better. Presently, only presidential campaigns are supported by public funding. It is quite likely, however, that the concept will be extended to congressional candidates and candidates for state office. If that does come to pass, and if there is some mechanism whereby campaigns would be able either to receive public funds early or to borrow early on expected receipts, the planning capability of the organization may increase. If campaign decision makers know they can rely on specific amounts, they may be able to allocate usage in a more rational manner than they are currently able to do. If a campaign knows, for instance, that it is going to have $15,000 to spend in the first month of its existence, chances are it will use the money for organizational purposes, such as hiring staff and planning fund-raising activities. This would be a reversal of the cash flow that campaigns usually encounter: most donors now give toward the end of a campaign, when the election is more visible. Money that comes in late cannot be used to build or sustain the organization; it is more likely to be used to buy more media time and other such expenses that require little or no staff work.

Fund-Raising Changes

Personal contact in fund raising will decrease, and mass approaches, such as direct mail campaigns and television appeals, will increase. The greater reliance on mass appeals will not affect campaign activity so much as it will the substance of campaigns: they will be directed to special interest groups, and they may well become more ideological.

People give money to a candidate in whom they believe (and to whom they may have special access), or because they believe in what that candidate stands for. Since a person who gives only a few dollars to a campaign will not have access to the candidate, the only reason for giving is because he or she supports something the giver cares deeply about. And those issues are usually divisive: abortion, ecology, war/peace, and so on.

Fund-raising events will, if not decline in number, at least increase in size to large-scale entertainment activities, such as rock concerts and celebrity appearances. Raising money in small amounts from large numbers of people is particularly appropriate when public funding is involved because small donations ($250 and less) will be matched. Although this approach is especially relevant in presidential campaigns, it is likely to be copied by smaller campaign organizations because they tend to follow the patterns set at the presidential level.

Campaign-Spending Changes

Disclosure requirements will tend to direct money to disclosable activities. Bookkeeping responsibilities may encourage campaign decision makers to invest in broadly visible activities, such as paid media advertising, large-scale fund-raising events, and so on. Most of those activities will not require much from the organization, particularly the volunteer organization, but they will seek to make the candidate more visible to the electorate.

Those who spend large portions of the campaign budget will have a greater role in decision making. Those who design and produce paid media advertising and direct mail campaigns will have an increasingly important role in deciding campaign strategy. Although fund raising will always be an important reason for relying on the advice of experts in these growing professions, their views of what appeals to voters will become more important. In recent years, campaigns have relied extensively on pollsters for that advice (and in the past, on party regulars). One potential difference between relying on pollsters on the one hand, and direct mail experts on the other hand, is that the former supply information about majority views and the latter focus on special interest views. Reliance on direct mail strategists may lead to more divisive campaigns.

There will be less spending in less visible areas. Such items as campaign brochures (exclusive of material sent through the mails), buttons, yard signs, and bumper stickers will dwindle in importance, if not disappear altogether. All of these materials were developed for, and used by, local field organizations. Since the field organizations will decline, so will these now common examples of campaign paraphernalia. Local organizations used to sell campaign buttons and bumper stickers to raise money. Given the complexity of record keeping and public financing, such sales will no longer be as cost-effective, and they may become illegal.

Changes in the Political Environment

Campaign reform may further separate candidates from parties. As one 1976 campaigner put it, "The law encourages candidates to stay away from other candidates in the party because of splitting costs and reporting procedures. We would have done much more for the party without the law than we did with the law."[6] The law in 1976 worked against activities that associated

---

[6]*Ibid.*, 50.

the candidate with either his party or other candidates of the party. There was the danger that someone outside the campaign organization would make a mistake and it would lead to a bad headline. There was the ruling of the FEC that precluded cooperative efforts, such as sharing a poster or bumper sticker. The problem is how costs are shared and how accounts are handled. (And when one of the candidates is publicly financed, there is the danger of exceeding spending limits or inadvertently "publicly financing" a candidate for office not legally financed with public money.)

Although operating separately from campaigns, parties may assume some significant roles in elections. Certain kinds of activities may be farmed out entirely to parties, particularly those in which they already play a partial role: voter identification and registration drives, and get-out-the-vote efforts. As permanent organizations, parties may be in a better position to maintain contributor lists, which have become essential to campaigns.

Parties may begin campaigning for themselves if they cannot campaign for candidates. We may see new types of campaign advertising, with parties advertising themselves without reference to candidates: "Vote Democratic" or "Vote Republican" posters and literature. Party organizations may be forced to take positions on issues or seek to regain control of the nominating process.

Independent spenders may enter the process. Individuals or groups who choose to support candidates but are not associated with the campaigns may come to play an important role in elections. Although independent spenders are required to be independent from candidates and campaigns, they are not required to be independent of each other. It is possible that there will be coalitions of independent spenders. It is likely that they will make such expenditures only for "hot" issues or ideological causes. From the campaign perspective, independent expenditures may end up causing more harm than good, because the people making them will be more intense and less aware either of the law or of the mores of campaigning.

Although campaign reform has undercut the influence of individuals, it may not have done away with the influence of special interests. As one 1976 campaigner noted, "I'm not convinced big money is out of politics. People who 'work' PAC's still have influence."[7] Coalitions of groups, albeit independent of campaigns, may well influence the substance of campaigns as candidates vie for their support. And, of course, it is also possible to organize groups to contribute to campaigns.

Conclusions

It seems inevitable that controls on campaigns will increase rather than decrease with time. There will be controls arising from reporting procedures and from rules governing acceptance of public funds. The debate on public financing has been waged principally at the federal level, but it will undoubtedly appear at the state level as well.

There is some concern that the controls themselves may become a threat to the freedom of the political process, that the government will start telling campaign organizations how they can spend their money, and that those who make such decisions will not be immune from self-interest. As long as the regulations are fairly applied to everyone, as they seem to have been thus far, there is probably little danger of corruption.[8] Another concern is that the requirements of reporting will become so complex and so burdensome to campaigns that the danger lies less in consciously working the system to benefit one side or the other, than in deadening campaign activity to the point that it excludes all but a very few highly skilled, technically trained participants.

The truth is that we really do not know very much at all about the impact of money on campaigns. These speculations are, after all, only speculations. We have some sense that money can make a difference in elections (particularly when one candidate is not well known),[9] but does it matter at the organizational level?

---

[7]*Ibid.*, 24.

[8]*Ibid.*, 52–53.

[9]Gary Jacobsen, "Practical Consequences of Campaign Finance Reform: An Incumbent Protection Act?" *Public Policy*, vol. 24, no. 1 (Winter 1976).

Public financing may lead to a more stable cash flow for the organization, which, in turn, may lead to a greater capacity to plan from the beginning. There are, however, two schools of thought on the subject: the first arguing that more money in the beginning (as a result of public financing) would go into organization building; the second arguing that more money at any time would be put into paid media advertising, and the organization would be no better off than it was before.[10] It is also possible that a stable cash flow would not change the dynamic of the organization in the least. As one 1976 campaigner put it, "The object is to win. And the psychology is to save. You have to try to get the maximum out of the money this week so that you're still around next week."[11] The most important factor in predicting or explaining campaign organization behavior is the impending election.

I repeat, however, that we do not know what difference more money, or more stable money, will make. And I would add that at this point we do not know what difference campaign reform in general will make. Disclosure of contributions and expenses may tell a great deal about a candidate's resources and use of those resources — but only if somebody reads them and lets voters know about it. So far, use of this public material has been minimal because it is kept in Washington and because it becomes too voluminous for all but the most intrepid to read.

Contribution and spending limits may put candidates on a more even basis in their capacity to reach voters, thereby assuring some form of political equality, but they will not be equal. One will have more visibility because of past activities, family association, or access to special interest groups of a larger size. One will have more visibility because his or her campaign is more creative at capturing the interest of the assignment editors in television news departments.

There is a limit to what reform can or should do. Perhaps the most potentially serious side effect of reform will be forcing campaigns to run more ideologically, making stronger appeals to special interest groups. Certainly there has been, and may

---

[10]Kayden, "Conference Report," 31–32; Decision Making Information and Hart Research Associates, "A Study of the Impact . . ."

[11]Kayden, "Conference Report," 30.

continue to be, a decline in the involvement of people who used to give because they wanted something special from the candidate. As one of the 1976 campaigners put it, "Today, contributing is not a way to participate, but a way to isolation."[12] More or less, that was the intent of the law. But those people had an investment in the political system as it is. People who are motivated by special interest or ideological concerns have a strong investment in change. The electoral process may become more combative as a result. That is something to observe carefully and to think about deeply.

---

[12]*Ibid.*, 21.

INDEX

1 2 3 4 5 6 7 8 9 10